SI(
(signs use

Good foot
(sufficiently distinct to be followed ....) ‒ ‒ ‒

Intermittent footpath   ‒ · ‒ · ‒ · ‒ · ‒ · ‒
(difficult to follow in mist)

Route recommended   ·· ‒ ‒ ·········· ‒ ‒ ····
    but no path
(if recommended one way only, arrow indicates direction)

Wall ∞∞∞∞∞∞∞∞   **Broken wall** ∘∘∘∘∘∘∘∘∘∘∘

Fence +++++++++++   **Broken fence** ıııııııııııııııı

Marshy ground ⯆⯆⯆⯆⯆   **Trees** 🌳🌳🌳🌳🌳

Crags 🪨🪨🪨   **Boulders** ◊◊◊◊◊

Stream or River
        (arrow indicates direction of flow)

Waterfall ‒⋀⋀‒   **Bridge** ~~~×~~~

Buildings ■■   **Unenclosed road** ⬚⬚⬚⬚⬚

Contours (at 100' intervals)
                    ···· 1900 ····
                    ···· 1800 ····
                    ···· 1700 ····

Summit-cairn ▲   **Other** (prominent) **cairns** △

Twelve Favourite Mountains

PICTORIAL GUIDES BY A. WAINWRIGHT

Book One: The Eastern Fells
Book Two: The Far Eastern Fells
Book Three: The Central Fells
Book Four: The Southern Fells
Book Five: The Northern Fells
Book Six: The North Western Fells
Book Seven: The Western Fells

The Outlying Fells of Lakeland
Pennine Way Companion
A Coast to Coast Walk

Walks on the Howgill Fells
Walks in Limestone Country

REVISED PICTORIAL GUIDES
BY A. WAINWRIGHT, REVISED BY CHRIS JESTY

Book One: The Eastern Fells Second Edition
Book Two: The Far Eastern Fells Second Edition
Book Three: The Central Fells Second Edition
Book Four: The Southern Fells Second Edition
Book Five: The Northern Fells Second Edition (Autumn 2007)
Book Six: The North Western Fells (in preparation)
Book Seven: The Western Fells Second Edition (in preparation)

OTHER BOOKS BY A. WAINWRIGHT

Fellwalking with Wainwright (photographs by Derry Brabbs)
Memoirs of a Fellwanderer
Pennine Journey
Lakeland Sketchbooks (five volumes)
Scottish Mountain Drawings (two volumes)
Westmorland Heritage

Twelve
Favourite
Mountains

by

a.wainwright

FRANCES LINCOLN

Frances Lincoln Limited, 4 Torriano Mews, Torriano Avenue,
London NW5 2RZ
www.franceslincoln.com

The Pictorial Guides to the Lakeland Fells first published by
Frances Lincoln 2003
This collection published by Frances Lincoln 2007

PUBLISHER'S NOTE
The core of this book consists of unamended pages from A. Wainwright's
Pictorial Guides. The maps and descriptions of walks reproduced here were
correct, to the best of A. Wainwright's knowledge, at the time they were first
published in the 1950s and 1960s, but the footpaths, cairns and waymarks
described here may have changed since then. Walkers are strongly advised to
check with an up-to-date map when planning a walk. They are also advised
to take sensible safety precautions when out on the fells.

A programme of revision of the Pictorial Guides is well under way and
revised editions of each book will continue to appear over the next few years.

The fells appear in the following Pictorial Guides:
Place Fell: *The Far Eastern Fells*
Harrison Stickle and Pike o' Stickle: *The Central Fells*
Bowfell, Crinkle Crags, Scafell and Scafell Pike: *The Southern Fells*
Blencathra and Carrock Fell: *The Northern Fells*
Great Gable, Haystacks and Pillar: *The Western Fells*

Printed and bound in China
A CIP catalogue record is available for this book from the British Library.

ISBN 978 0 7112 2820 7
9 8 7 6 5 4 3 2 1

Contents

The Twelve Mountains

above: Wainwright dressed for fell walking

I promised to give my opinion of the six best fells. I should not have used the word 'best', which suggests that some are not as good as others. I think they are all good. The finest, however, must have the attributes of mountains, i.e., height, a commanding appearance, a good view, steepness and ruggedness: qualities that are most pronounced in the volcanic area of the south-western sector. I now give, after much biting of finger-nails, what I consider to be the finest half-dozen:

SCAFELL PIKE
BOWFELL
PILLAR
GREAT GABLE
BLENCATHRA
CRINKLE CRAGS

These are not necessarily the six fells I like best. It grieves me to have to omit Haystacks (most of all), Langdale Pikes, Place Fell, Carrock Fell and some others simply because they do not measure up in altitude to the grander mountains. There will be surprise at the omission of Scafell, the crags of which provide the finest sight in Lakeland, but too much of this fell is lacking in interest. It would be seventh if there were seven in the list. Contrary to general opinion (which would favour Great Gable), the grandest of the lot is Scafell Pike. Of the six, all are of volcanic rock with the exception of Blencathra.

INTRODUCTION

Surely there is no other place in this whole wonderful world quite like Lakeland ...no other so exquisitely lovely, no other so charming, no other that calls so insistently across a gulf of distance. All who truly love Lakeland are exiles when away from it.

Here, in small space, is the wonderland of childhood's dreams, lingering far beyond childhood through the span of a man's life: its enchantment grows with passing years and quiet eventide is enriched by the haunting sweetness of dear memories, memories that remain evergreen through the flight of time, that refresh and sustain in the darker days. How many, these memories..........the moment of wakening, and the sudden joyful realisation that this is to be another day of freedom on the hills........ the dawn chorus of bird-song........ the delicate lacework of birches against the sky ...... morning sun drawing aside the veils of mist; black-stockinged lambs, in springtime, amongst the daffodils......... silver cascades dancing and leaping down bracken steeps..... autumn colours ......a red fox running over snow....... the silence of lonely hills...... storm and tempest in the high places, and the unexpected glimpses of valleys dappled in sunlight far beneath the swirling clouds............rain, and the intimate shelter of lichened walls........fierce winds on the heights and soft breezes that are no more than gentle caresses..........a sheepdog watching its master

.... the snow and ice and freezing stillnesses of midwinter : a white world, rosy-pink as the sun goes down ....the supreme moment when the top cairn comes into sight at last, only minutes away, after the long climb ....the small ragged sheep that brave the blizzards .... the symphonies of murmuring streams, unending, with never a discord ......curling smoke from the chimneys of the farm down below amongst the trees, where the day shall end ......oil-lamps in flagged kitchens, huge fires in huge fireplaces, huge suppers ....glittering moonlight on placid waters ......stars above dark peaks.....the tranquillity that comes before sleep, when thoughts are of the day that is gone and the day that is to come .... All these memories, and so many more, breathing anew the rare quality and magical atmosphere of Lakeland ......memories that belong to Lakeland, and could not belong in the same way to any other place.............. memories that enslave the mind forever.

Many are they who have fallen under the spell of Lakeland, and many are they who have been moved to tell of their affection, in story and verse and picture and song.

This book is one man's way of expressing his devotion to Lakeland's friendly hills. It was conceived, and is born, after many years of inarticulate worshipping at their shrines.

It is, in very truth, a love-letter.

Classification and Definition

Any division of the Lakeland fells into geographical districts must necessarily be arbitrary, just as the location of the outer boundaries of Lakeland must always be a matter of opinion. Any attempt to define internal or external boundaries is certain to invite criticism, and he who takes it upon himself to say where Lakeland starts and finishes, or, for example, where the Central Fells merge into the Southern Fells and *which* fells are the Central Fells and which the Southern and *why* they need be so classified, must not expect his pronouncements to be generally accepted.

Yet for present purposes some plan of classification and definition must be used. County and parochial boundaries are no help, nor is the recently-defined area of the Lakeland National Park, for this book is concerned only with the high ground.

First, the external boundaries.   Straight lines linking the extremities of the outlying lakes enclose all the higher fells very conveniently. There are a few fells of lesser height to the north and east, however, that are typically Lakeland in character and cannot properly be omitted : these are brought in, somewhat untidily, by extending the lines in those areas. Thus :

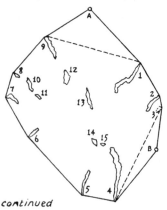

1 : *Ullswater*
2 : *Hawes Water*
3 : proposed *Swindale Resr*
4 : *Windermere*
5 : *Coniston Water*
6 : *Wast Water*
7 : *Ennerdale Water*
8 : *Loweswater*
9 : *Bassenthwaite Lake*
10 : *Crummock Water*
11 : *Buttermere*
12 : *Derwent Water*
13 : *Thirlmere*
14 : *Grasmere*
15 : *Rydal Water*
A : *Caldbeck*
B : *Longsleddale (church)*

continued

Classification and Definition

continued
    The complete Guide is planned to include
all the fells in the area enclosed by the straight lines
of the diagram. This is an undertaking quite beyond
the compass of a single volume, and it is necessary,
therefore, to divide the area into convenient sections,
making the fullest use of natural boundaries (lakes,
valleys and low passes) so that each district is, as far
as possible, self-contained and independent of the rest.

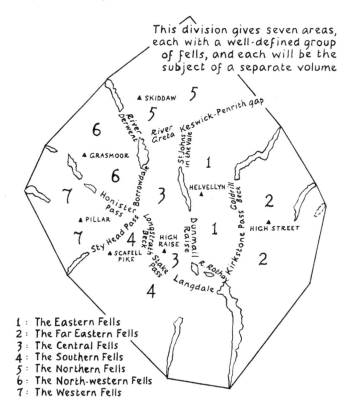

This division gives seven areas,
each with a well-defined group
of fells, and each will be the
subject of a separate volume

1: The Eastern Fells
2: The Far Eastern Fells
3: The Central Fells
4: The Southern Fells
5: The Northern Fells
6: The North-western Fells
7: The Western Fells

INTRODUCTION

Notes on the Illustrations

THE MAPS .... Many excellent books have been written about Lakeland, but the best literature of all for the walker is that published by the Director General of Ordnance Survey, the 1" map for companionship and guidance on expeditions, the 2½" map for exploration both on the fells and by the fireside. These admirable maps are remarkably accurate topographically but there is a crying need for a revision of the paths on the hills: several walkers' tracks that have come into use during the past few decades, some of them now broad highways, are not shown at all; other paths still shown on the maps have fallen into neglect and can no longer be traced on the ground.

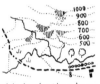

The popular Bartholomew 1" map is a beautiful picture, fit for a frame, but this too is unreliable for paths; indeed here the defect is much more serious, for routes are indicated where no paths ever existed, nor ever could — the cartographer has preferred to take precipices in his stride rather than deflect his graceful curves over easy ground.

Hence the justification for the maps in this book: they have the one merit (of importance to walkers) of being dependable as regards delineation of *paths*. They are intended as supplements to the Ordnance Survey maps, certainly not as substitutes.

THE VIEWS .... Various devices have been used to illustrate the views from the summits of the fells. The full panorama in the form of an outline drawing is most satisfactory generally, and this method has been adopted for the main viewpoints.

THE DIAGRAMS OF ASCENTS .... The routes of ascent of the higher fells are depicted by diagrams that do not pretend to strict accuracy: they are neither plans nor elevations; in fact there is deliberate distortion in order to show detail clearly: usually they are represented as viewed from imaginary 'space-stations.' But it is hoped they will be useful and interesting.

THE DRAWINGS .... The drawings at least are honest attempts to reproduce what the eye sees: they illustrate features of interest and also serve the dual purpose of breaking up the text and balancing the layout of the pages, and of filling up awkward blank spaces, like this:

TWELVE FAVOURITE MOUNTAINS
from The Pictorial Guides to the Lakeland Fells

Blencathra

2847'

MUNGRISDALE 2
HESKET NEWMARKET 9

*from
Mungrisdale road end*

better known,
unfortunately,
as Saddleback

BOWSCALE FELL ▲
SKIDDAW ▲   Mungrisdale ●
● Skiddaw
House   SOUTHER FELL ▲
▲ BLENCATHRA
LONSCALE ▲
FELL ● Scales
● Threlkeld

MILES
0 1 2 3 4

NATURAL FEATURES

Blencathra is one of the grandest objects in Lakeland. And one of the best known. Seen from the south-west, the popular aspect, the mountain rises steeply and in isolation above the broad green fields of Threlkeld, a feature being the great sweeping curve leaping out of the depths to a lofty summit-ridge, where the skyline then proceeds in a succession of waves to a sharp peak before descending, again in a graceful curve, to the valley pastures far to the east.

This is a mountain that compels attention, even from those dull people whose eyes are not habitually lifted to the hills. To artists and photographers it is an obvious subject for their craft; to sightseers passing along the road or railway at its base, between Keswick and Penrith, its influence is magnetic; to the dalesfolk it is the eternal background to their lives, there at birth, there at death. But most of all it is a mountaineers' mountain.

continued

from Castlerigg Stone Circle

NATURAL FEATURES

continued

The supreme feature of Blencathra, the one that invests the mountain with special grandeur, is the imposing southern front, a remarkable example of the effect of elemental natural forces. It forms a tremendous facade above the valley, and makes a dark, towering backcloth to a stage of farmsteads and cottages, of emerald pastures and meadows and woodlands along its base. There is nothing inviting in these shattered cliffs and petrified rivers of stone that seem to hold a perpetual threat over the little community below : the scene arrests attention, but intimidates and repels. Few who gaze upon these desolate walls are likely to feel any inclination and inspiration to scramble up through their arid, stony wildernesses to the contorted skyline so high above. Consequently the area has remained a no-man's-land for walkers, even though closely within sight of road and railway travellers. Blencathra is ascended thousands of times a year but rarely by ways up the southern front. This is a pity. Here is the greatness of the mountain. Its detail is a fascinating study.

west   east

THE SOUTHERN FRONT
3¼ miles

The outer slopes, rising on the west and east flanks from valley level to the uppermost escarpment below the summit ridge, are smoothly curved, massive and yet so symmetrical that they might well have been designed by a master architect to supply a perfect balance to the structure. These two outlyers are Blease Fell and Scales Fell.

Blease Fell   Scales Fell

continued

NATURAL FEATURES

continued

From their extremities the slopes of Blease Fell and Scales Fell extend uneventfully towards each other across the front until, suddenly and dramatically, they are halted at the edge of a scene of devastation, the wreckage of what appears to have been, in ages past, a tremendous convulsion that tore the heart out of the mountain and left the ruins seemingly in a state of tottering collapse. The picture is chaotic: a great upheaval of ridges and pinnacles rising out of dead wastes of scree and penetrated by choked gullies and ravines, the whole crazily tilted through 2000' of altitude. Even in this area of confusion and disorder, however, Nature has sculptured a distinct pattern.

Four watercourses emerge from surrounding debris to escape to the valley:

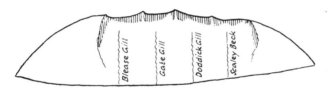

Between the four ravines, three lofty spurs, alike in main characteristics, thrust far out; narrow and frail where they leave the solid mass of the mountain, they widen into substantial buttresses as they descend to the valley. It is as though a giant hand had clawed at the mountain, each finger scooping out a deep hollow, with narrow strips of ground left undisturbed between.

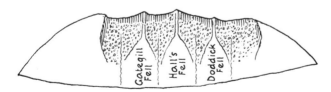

There are thus five buttresses on the southern front, each named as a separate fell. The two outer are grassy, with flat tops; the three in the middle are heathery and rise to distinct peaks, the central one being Blencathra's summit. Such is the pattern of the southern front.

continued

NATURAL FEATURES

continued

The other flanks of the mountain are mainly smooth and rounded, although on the east side Scales Fell breaks its curve to form the hollow of Mousthwaite Combe. But, from the summit, high ground continues north across a slight depression ('the Saddle) to the prominent top of Foule Crag, this being the outline from which the alternative name, Saddleback, derives. A distinct ridge curves away to the Glenderamackin col from Foule Crag, while a rocky spur goes off to the east, this latter being the well-known Sharp Edge, second in fame to Striding Edge on Helvellyn as a test for walkers. Deepset in the hollow between Sharp Edge and the main ridge is one of the most characteristic mountain tarns in the district, Scales Tarn.

It is interesting to note that although Blencathra lies well to the east of the axis of Lakeland, approximately 99% of its drainage joins the Derwent in the west, only a few drops being gathered by the Eden catchment.

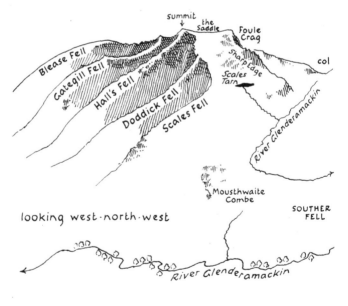

looking west·north·west

Blencathra joins Bowfell in the author's best half-dozen.

The summit escarpment

looking
west

from
Scales Fell
to the
summit

from
the summit
to Gategill
Fell Top

from
Gategill
Fell Top
to
Blease Fell

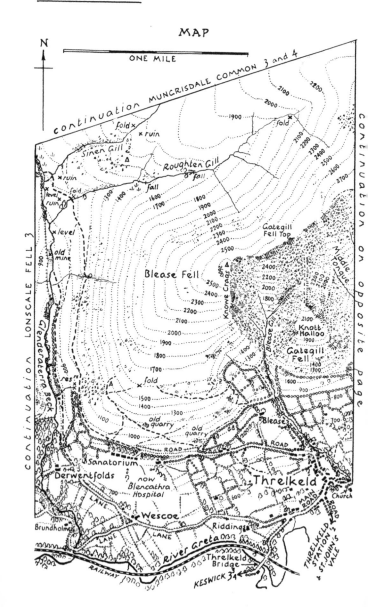

MAP

ONE MILE

N

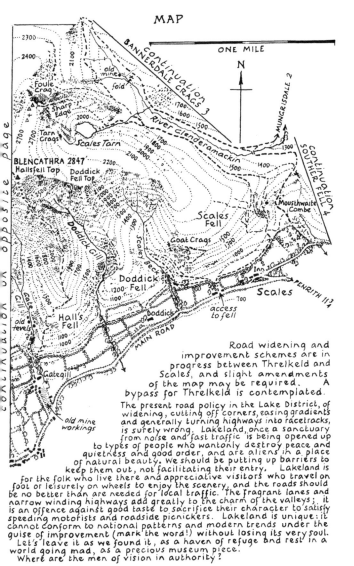

MAP

ONE MILE

N

Road widening and improvement schemes are in progress between Threlkeld and Scales, and slight amendments of the map may be required. A bypass for Threlkeld is contemplated.

The present road policy in the Lake District, of widening, cutting off corners, easing gradients and generally turning highways into racetracks, is surely wrong. Lakeland, once a sanctuary from noise and fast traffic is being opened up to types of people who wantonly destroy peace and quietness and good order, and are aliens in a place of natural beauty. We should be putting up barriers to keep them out, not facilitating their entry. Lakeland is for the folk who live there and appreciative visitors who travel on foot or leisurely on wheels to enjoy the scenery, and the roads should be no better than are needed for local traffic. The fragrant lanes and narrow winding highways add greatly to the charm of the valleys; it is an offence against good taste to sacrifice their character to satisfy speeding motorists and roadside picnickers. Lakeland is unique: it cannot conform to national patterns and modern trends under the guise of improvement (mark the word!) without losing its very soul.

Let's leave it as we found it, as a haven of refuge and rest in a world going mad, as a precious museum piece.

Where are the men of vision in authority?

ASCENT FROM THRELKELD
via ROUGHTEN GILL
2400 feet of ascent : 5 miles

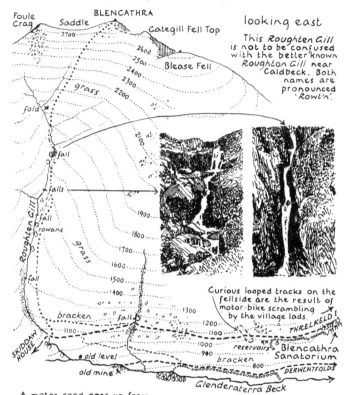

looking east

Foule Crag
Saddle
2700
BLENCATHRA
Gategill Fell Top
2600
2500
2400
2300
2200
Blease Fell
grass

fold ✗

fall
falls
fall
rowans

Roughten Gill
grass
2100
1900
1800
1700
1600
1500
1400
1300
1200
1100
1000
990
800

fall

bracken
fall

SKIDDAW HOUSE

old level
old mine

reservoirs
bracken

THRELKELD
Blencathra Sanatorium
DERWENTFOLDS

Glenderaterra Beck

This *Roughten Gill* is not to be confused with the better known *Roughton Gill* near Caldbeck. Both names are pronounced 'Rowt'n'.

Curious looped tracks on the fellside are the result of motor-bike scrambling by the village lads.

A motor-road goes up from Threlkeld to the Sanatorium and ends there. Its direction is continued by a wide grass path (gate in fence) along the side of the Sanatorium wall. Use this.

For walkers who panic at the proximity of precipices and cannot face steep slopes, the roundabout route by Roughten Gill, which holds no terrors at all, is a good way to the top, but most people will find it unexciting and dreary. The best thing about it is delayed until the very end: the sudden thrilling view of Lakeland, which has been hidden during the climb.

ASCENT FROM THRELKELD
via BLEASE FELL
2450 feet of ascent : 2½ miles

looking north
Blease Fell

Gategill
Fell Top

BLENCATHRA

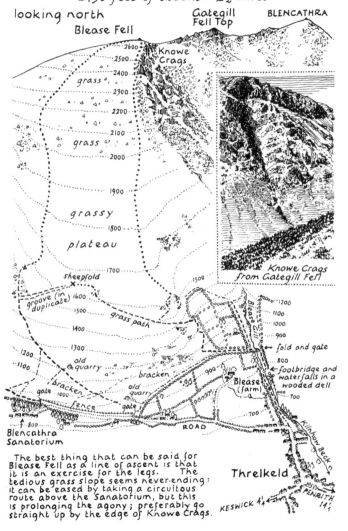

Knowe
Crags

2600
2500
2400
grass
2300
2200
2100
grass
2000

1900

grassy

1800

plateau

1700

sheepfold
×

groove (in
duplicate)
1600
grass path
1500
1400
1300
old
quarry
bracken
old
quarry
1200
1100
bracken
gate 1000
fence
gate
800
Blencathra
Sanatorium

ROAD

1500

1200
1100
1000
900
fold and gate
800
footbridge and
waterfalls in a
wooded dell

Blease
(farm)

900

700

Blease Gill

Kinbow Beck

Knowe Crags
from Gategill Fell

Threlkeld

KESWICK 4¼

PENRITH
14¼

The best thing that can be said for
Blease Fell as a line of ascent is that
it is an exercise for the legs.   The
tedious grass slope seems never-ending:
it can be eased by taking a circuitous
route above the Sanatorium, but this
is prolonging the agony; preferably go
straight up by the edge of Knowe Crags.

Blease Gill

ASCENT FROM THRELKELD
via BLEASE GILL
2400 feet of ascent : 2 miles

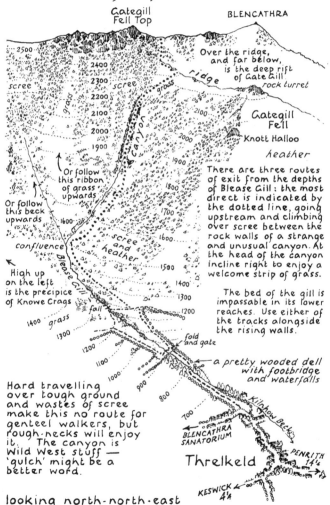

Gategill Fell Top

BLENCATHRA

2500

2400
2300
2200
2100
2000
1900

scree

grass

scree

grass

ridge

Over the ridge, and far below, is the deep rift of Gate Gill

rock turret

2100

Gategill Fell

2000

Knott Halloo

heather

1900

Or follow this ribbon of grass upwards

1800

Or follow this beck upwards

1600

1700

scree and heather

1600

confluence

There are three routes of exit from the depths of Blease Gill: the most direct is indicated by the dotted line, going upstream and climbing over scree between the rock walls of a strange and unusual canyon. At the head of the canyon incline right to enjoy a welcome strip of grass.

1500

High up on the left is the precipice of Knowe Crags

1400

1300

The bed of the gill is impassable in its lower reaches. Use either of the tracks alongside the rising walls.

1400

grass

1300

fall

1200

1200

1100

fold and gate

a pretty wooded dell with footbridge and waterfalls

900

800

Kilnhow Beck

Hard travelling over tough ground and wastes of scree make this no route for genteel walkers, but rough-necks will enjoy it.   The canyon is Wild West stuff — 'gulch' might be a better word.

700

BLENCATHRA SANATORIUM

Threlkeld

PENRITH 14½

KESWICK 4½

looking north-north-east

ASCENT FROM THRELKELD
via GATEGILL FELL
2450 feet of ascent : 2 miles

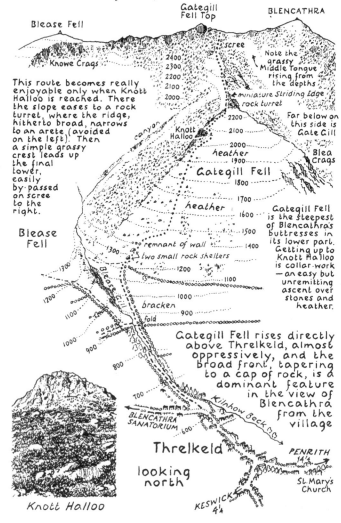

Blease Fell

Gategill Fell Top

BLENCATHRA

Knowe Crags

Note the grassy Middle Tongue rising from the depths

scree

2400
2300
2200
2100
2000

miniature Striding Edge rock turret

This route becomes really enjoyable only when Knott Halloo is reached. There the slope eases to a rock turret, where the ridge, hitherto broad, narrows to an arete (avoided on the left). Then a simple grassy crest leads up the final tower, easily by-passed on scree to the right.

2200
2100
2000
1900

Knott Halloo

heather

canyon

Far below on this side is Gate Gill

Blea Crags

Gategill Fell

1800

Blease Fell

heather

1700
1600
1500
1400

Gategill Fell is the steepest of Blencathra's buttresses in its lower part. Getting up to Knott Halloo is collar-work — an easy but unremitting ascent over stones and heather.

1300

remnant of wall

two small rock shelters

1200

1100

Blease Gill

1200

1100

1000

bracken

900

fold

1000

900

800

Gategill Fell rises directly above Threlkeld, almost oppressively, and the broad front, tapering to a cap of rock, is a dominant feature in the view of Blencathra from the village

700

Kilnhow Beck

BLENCATHRA SANATORIUM

600

Threlkeld

looking north

PENRITH 14½

St. Mary's Church

KESWICK 4½

Knott Halloo

looking up to Gategill Fell Top from just above Knott Halloo, with the rock turret on the right

Gategill Fell

looking up the ridge from the rock turret

looking down the ridge from Gategill Fell Top

The rock turret is at the far end of the shadow; to the right is Knott Halloo, the furthest point in view.

Gate Gill

Blencathra's summit is directly ahead.
Gategill Fell rises on the left, and
Hall's Fell on the right.

ASCENT FROM THRELKELD
via MIDDLE TONGUE
2400 feet of ascent : 2 miles

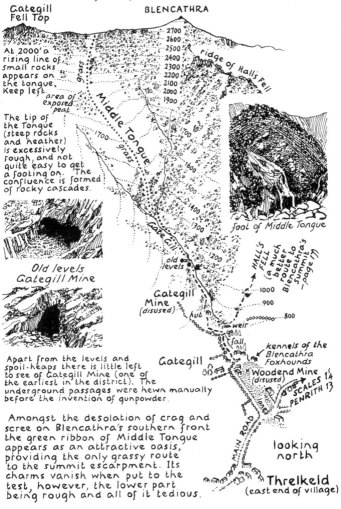

Gategill
Fell Top

BLENCATHRA

2700
2600
2500
2400
2300
2200
2100
2000
1900

ridge of Hall's Fell

At 2000' a
rising line of
small rocks
appears on
the tongue.
Keep left.

area of
exposed
peat

Middle Tongue

grass

grass

The tip of
the Tongue
(steep rocks
and heather)
is excessively
rough, and not
quite easy to get
a footing on. The
confluence is formed
of rocky cascades.

1700

1700

1600

1500

1300

foot of Middle Tongue

Old levels
Gategill Mine

Gategill

old
levels

1200

HALL'S FELL
(a much
better
route to
Blencathra's
summit
— page 17)

1000

900

800

Gategill
Mine
(disused)

hut

weir

fall

kennels of the
Blencathra
Foxhounds

Gategill

Woodend Mine
(disused)

SCALES 1¼
PENRITH 13

Apart from the levels and
spoil-heaps there is little left
to see of Gategill Mine (one of
the earliest in the district). The
underground passages were hewn manually
before the invention of gunpowder.

Amongst the desolation of crag and
scree on Blencathra's southern front
the green ribbon of Middle Tongue
appears as an attractive oasis,
providing the only grassy route
to the summit escarpment. Its
charms vanish when put to the
test, however, the lower part
being rough and all of it tedious.

MAIN ROAD

looking
north

Threlkeld
(east end of village)

ASCENT FROM THRELKELD
via HALL'S FELL
2400 feet of ascent : 2 miles

Gategill Fell Top

BLENCATHRA (Hallsfell Top)

Doddick Fell Top

The last half-mile of the ridge, from 2000', is entirely delightful. This section, known as Narrow Edge with good reason, is a succession of low crags, with steps and gateways and towers of rock. A distinct track on grass is available for walkers — at first this keeps mostly on the Doddick side and later prefers the other, occasionally being forced along the crest. Care is needed in places but there are no difficulties. Scramblers will enjoy following the crest throughout.

Under ice and snow the ridge is for experts only

An enchanting track climbs the broad base of the fell. Unseen from below, this track reveals itself in the heather a few yards at a time, beckoning irresistibly upwards to the exciting ridge above.

For active walkers and scramblers, this route is *positively* the finest way to any mountain-top in the district. It is direct, exhilarating, has glorious views, and (especially satisfying) scores a bull's-eye by leading unerringly to the summit-cairn.

arête
pinnacle
tower

care needed in traversing rockface by horizontal crack

From the ridge there are tremendous views down to Doddick and Gate Gills

Middle Tongue

Gategill Fell

heather

Doddick Gill

Doddick Fell and Scales Fell come into view

Hall's Fell

Doddick Fell

heather

bracken

Gate Gill

level

Gategill Mine (disused)

hut

weir

fold

fall

Gategill
kennels (the home of the Blencathra Foxhounds)

Woodend Mine (disused)
spoil heaps

SCALES 1¼
PENRITH 13

THRELKELD HALL (from which Hall's Fell is named)

MAIN ROAD

looking north

Threlkeld (east end of village)

looking down the ridge from the summit

Hall's Fell

the middle section

the curve in the ridge

looking up the ridge to the summit

Doddick Gill

from 1350' on Doddick Fell. On the left is Hall's Fell, rising to Hall's Fell Top (the summit of Blencathra).

ASCENT FROM THRELKELD
via DODDICK GILL
2150 feet of ascent : 2¾ miles

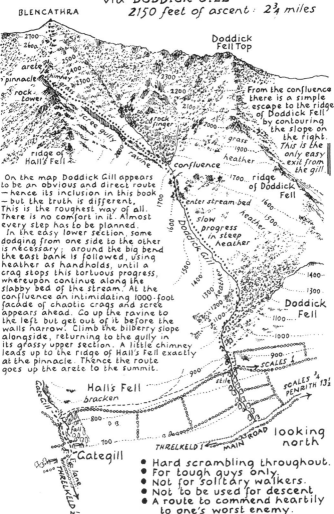

BLENCATHRA

2700
2600
arete
pinnacle
chimney
2500
2400
2300
rock tower
grass
scree gully
ridge of Hall's Fell
ravine

Doddick Fell Top
2300
2200
2100
rock finger

From the confluence there is a simple escape to the ridge of Doddick Fell by contouring the slope on the right. This is the only easy exit from the gill.

grass
1900
heather
confluence
1700   ridge of Doddick Fell
enter stream-bed
1800
slow progress in steep heather
heather
1600
1500

On the map Doddick Gill appears to be an obvious and direct route — hence its inclusion in this book — but the truth is different. This is the roughest way of all. There is no comfort in it. Almost every step has to be planned.

In the easy lower section, some dodging from one side to the other is necessary; around the big bend the east bank is followed, using heather as handholds, until a crag stops this tortuous progress, whereupon continue along the slabby bed of the stream. At the confluence an intimidating 1000-foot façade of chaotic crags and scree appears ahead. Go up the ravine to the left but get out of it before the walls narrow. Climb the bilberry slope alongside, returning to the gully in its grassy upper section. A little chimney leads up to the ridge of Hall's Fell exactly at the pinnacle. Thence the route goes up the arete to the summit.

1700
1600
1500
1400
1300
1200
1100
heather
Doddick Gill
1400
1300
Doddick Fell
1100
1000
900
SCALES ¼
stile
SCALES ¾
PENRITH 13½

Hall's Fell
bracken
Gategill Fell
800
700
fall
Gategill
lane   THRELKELD 2

THRELKELD 1   MAIN ROAD   looking north

- Hard scrambling throughout.
- For tough guys only.
- Not for solitary walkers.
- Not to be used for descent.
- A route to commend heartily to one's worst enemy.

ASCENT FROM SCALES
via DODDICK FELL
2150 feet of ascent: 1¾ miles

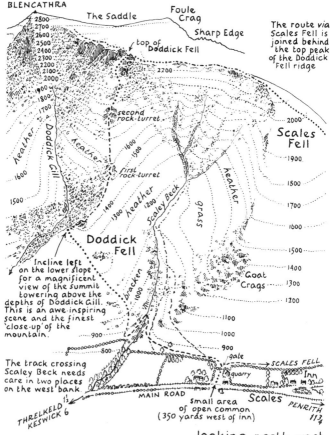

BLENCATHRA

2800
2700
2600
2500
2400
2300
2200
2100
2000

The Saddle

Foule Crag

Sharp Edge

top of Doddick Fell

The route via Scales Fell is joined behind the top peak of the Doddick Fell ridge

2200

second rock-turret

2000

Scales Fell

1900

1900
1800
1700
1600

Doddick Gill

heather

heather

1500

first rock-turret

heather

1800

heather

1700

1500

Doddick Fell

1400

1300

heather

1200

Scaley Beck

grass

1600

1500

1400

Goat Crags

1300

1200

Incline left on the lower slope for a magnificent view of the summit towering above the depths of Doddick Gill. This is an awe-inspiring scene and the finest 'close-up' of the mountain.

bracken

1100

1000

1100

1000

900

900

The track crossing Scaley Beck needs care in two places on the west bank.

800

gate

SCALES FELL

quarry

Inn

MAIN ROAD

Scales

THRELKELD
KESWICK 6

small area of open common (350 yards west of inn)

PENRITH
11¾

looking north-west

It is usual, from Scales, to ascend by way of Scales Fell, a very popular route, but better by far is the more direct ridge of Doddick Fell, a grand climb, quite easy, with striking views of the objective.
This is a splendid way to the top of Blencathra.

looking up to Doddick Fell Top from 1450'

Doddick Fell

looking down the ridge from Doddick Fell Top

Scaley Beck

Doddick Fell is on the left, rising to the peak of Doddick Fell Top.   Blencathra's summit is seen in the top left corner.

ASCENT FROM SCALES
via SCALEY BECK
2150 feet of ascent : 2 miles

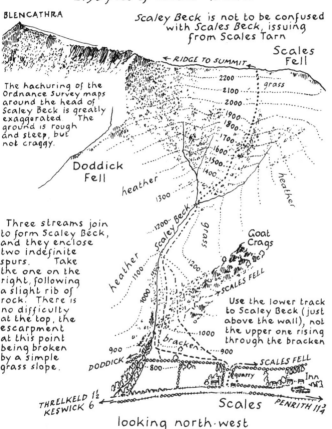

BLENCATHRA

Scaley Beck is not to be confused with Scales Beck, issuing from Scales Tarn

Scales Fell

← RIDGE TO SUMMIT →

grass

2200
2100
2000
1900
1800
1700
1600
1500
1400

The hachuring of the Ordnance Survey maps around the head of Scaley Beck is greatly exaggerated. The ground is rough and steep, but not craggy.

Doddick Fell

heather

1300

heather

Three streams join to form Scaley Beck, and they enclose two indefinite spurs. Take the one on the right, following a slight rib of rock. There is no difficulty at the top, the escarpment at this point being broken by a simple grass slope.

Scaley Beck

1200

1200

grass

Goat Crags

heather

1100

1000

SCALES FELL

Use the lower track to Scaley Beck (just above the wall), not the upper one rising through the bracken

1000

bracken

900

DODDICK

900

800

SCALES FELL

quarry

Inn

THRELKELD 1½
KESWICK 6

Scales

PENRITH 11½

looking north-west

Of the various watercourses on the south front Scaley Beck is the most practicable as a route of ascent, being nowhere too rough to stop progress; the exit, too, is easy. There is little of interest, however, and the route falls far short of that via the adjacent ridge of Doddick Fell.

ASCENT FROM SCALES
via SHARP EDGE
2250 feet of ascent : 2¼ miles

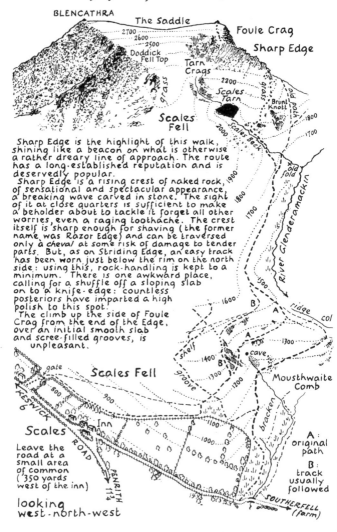

Sharp Edge is the highlight of this walk, shining like a beacon on what is otherwise a rather dreary line of approach. The route has a long-established reputation and is deservedly popular.

Sharp Edge is a rising crest of naked rock, of sensational and spectacular appearance, a breaking wave carved in stone. The sight of it at close quarters is sufficient to make a beholder about to tackle it forget all other worries, even a raging toothache. The crest itself is sharp enough for shaving (the former name was Razor Edge) and can be traversed only à cheval at some risk of damage to tender parts. But, as on Striding Edge, an easy track has been worn just below the rim on the north side: using this, rock-handling is kept to a minimum. There is one awkward place, calling for a shuffle off a sloping slab on to a knife-edge: countless posteriors have imparted a high polish to this spot.

The climb up the side of Foule Crag from the end of the Edge, over an initial smooth slab and scree-filled grooves, is unpleasant.

Leave the road at a small area of common (350 yards west of the inn)

looking west-north-west

A: original path

B: track usually followed

looking down from Foule Crag

looking east along the Edge (the 'awkward place' in the foreground)

Sharp Edge

the approach from Scales Tarn

from Scales Tarn

Foule Crag
Sharp Edge
Brunt Knott

the path from Scales

ASCENT FROM SCALES
via SCALES FELL
2150 feet of ascent · 2¼ miles

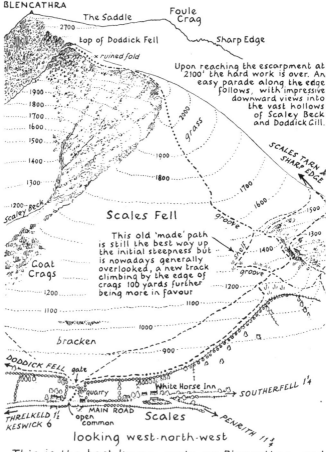

BLENCATHRA

The Saddle   Foule Crag

2700

top of Doddick Fell   Sharp Edge

× ruined fold

Upon reaching the escarpment at 2100' the hard work is over. An easy parade along the edge follows, with impressive downward views into the vast hollows of Scaley Beck and Doddick Gill.

1900
1800
1700
1600
1500
1400
1300
1200 Scaley Beck

2000

grass

1900

1800

1700

1600

1500

SCALES TARN
SHARP EDGE

Scales Fell

This old 'made' path is still the best way up the initial steepness but is nowadays generally overlooked, a new track climbing by the edge of crags 100 yards further being more in favour

groove

shelf

1400

groove

1300

1200

Coat Crags

1200

1100

1100

1100

1000

bracken

900

DODDICK FELL   gate

quarry   White Horse Inn   → SOUTHERFELL 1¼

THRELKELD 1½   MAIN ROAD
KESWICK 6   open common   Scales   PENRITH 11¾

looking west·north·west

This is the best-known route up Blencathra, and has been in common use for over a century. Even so, the tough grass of Scales Fell has resisted the formation of a continuous track. The climb, tedious up to 2000', becomes excellent in its later stages.

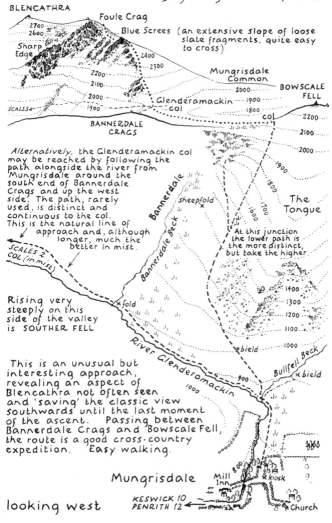

ASCENT FROM MUNGRISDALE
2250 feet of ascent : 4 miles

BLENCATHRA

Foule Crag

Blue Screes (an extensive slope of loose slate fragments, quite easy to cross)

2700
2600

Sharp Edge

2400

2300

Mungrisdale Common

2200

2100

2000

BOWSCALE FELL

2000

1900

SCALES

Glenderamackin col

1900

1800

col

1900

2200

BANNERDALE CRAGS

2100

2000

Alternatively, the Glenderamackin col may be reached by following the path alongside the river from Mungrisdale around the south end of Bannerdale Crags and up the west side. The path, rarely used, is distinct and continuous to the col. This is the natural line of approach and, although longer, much the better in mist.

Bannerdale

sheepfold

1900

1800

1700

1600

The Tongue

At this junction the lower path is the more distinct, but take the higher

SCALES 2 COL (in mist)

Bannerdale Beck

1400

1300

1200

1100

Rising very steeply on this side of the valley is SOUTHER FELL

×fold

1000

This is an unusual but interesting approach, revealing an aspect of Blencathra not often seen and 'saving' the classic view southwards until the last moment of the ascent. Passing between Bannerdale Crags and Bowscale Fell, the route is a good cross-country expedition. Easy walking.

River Glenderamackin

×bield

Bullfell Beck

×bield

900

1000

Mungrisdale

Mill Inn

×kiosk

looking west

KESWICK 10
PENRITH 12

Church

THE VIEW

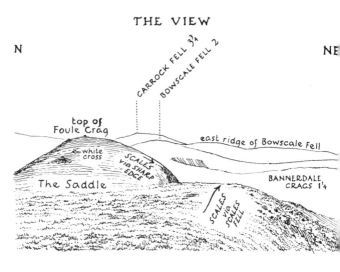

N

NE

CARROCK FELL 3¾

BOWSCALE FELL 2

top of
Foule Crag

white
cross

SCALES
VIA SHARP
EDGE

The Saddle

east ridge of Bowscale Fell

BANNERDALE
CRAGS 1¼

SCALES
VIA
SCALES
FELL

Hallsfell Top

THE SUMMIT

The summit is effectively poised above the abyss, precisely at the point where the ridge of Hall's Fell comes up out of the depths to a jutting headland. The summit is, in fact, known as Hallsfell Top. Much slaty stone is lying exposed here, but it is small stuff unsuitable for building imposing cairns, and nothing marks the highest point but a poor untidy heap of rubble; on occasion attempts are made to give the thing some shape and dignity but until somebody carries up a few decent-sized blocks the cairn will continue to disappoint by its insignificance.

The summit is windswept and shelterless and lacks a natural seat, but a few yards down Hall's Fell on the left the lee-side of a small outcrop usually cuts off the prevailing wind.

The excellent turf along the top deserves special mention.

continued

THE VIEW

NE   E

The Pennines in the background   Cross
                                         Fell

The Eden Valley   Penrith

                         SOUTHER
                         FELL 2

Mungrisdale

south ridge of
Bannerdale Crags

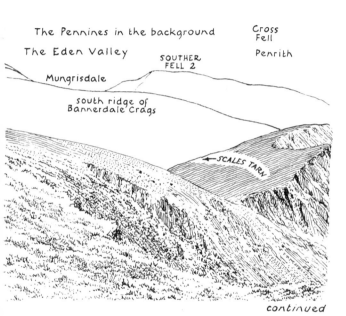

←SCALES TARN

continued

Descents:

The best *ascents* are by the narrow ridges —— Hall's Fell,
Sharp Edge, Doddick Fell and Gategill Fell, *in that order* ——
but the best routes of *descent* are those tedious in ascent:
Blease Fell, Scales Fell, Glenderamackin col and Roughten
Gill, *in that order*. The latter two are roundabout and not
suitable in mist, but Blease Fell and Scales Fell, lying at
opposite ends of the well-defined summit escarpment, are
simple ways off in any weather. The narrow ridges will be
found bumpy going down, although Hall's Fell and Doddick
Fell are quite practicable and enjoyable, but all may become
dangerous under ice and snow.   The gills and ravines on
the southern front are much too rough to be considered for
descent no matter how good the weather.

THE VIEW

continued

E   SE

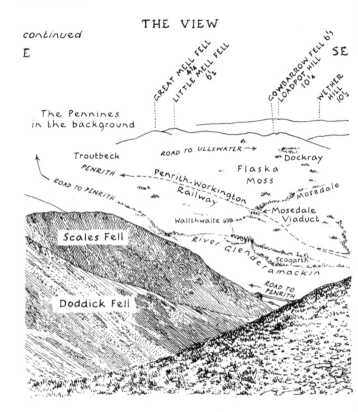

GREAT MELL FELL 4½
LITTLE MELL FELL 6½

GOWBARROW FELL 6½
LOADPOT HILL 10¼
WETHER HILL 10½

The Pennines
in the background

Troutbeck   *ROAD TO ULLSWATER →*   Dockray

PENRITH ←   Penrith-Workington   Flaska
                                                         Moss
ROAD TO PENRITH   Railway   Mosedale

                                              Mosedale
                                              Viaduct

Wallthwaite

Scales Fell   *River Glenderamackin*

                                                    Scogarth

Doddick Fell   ← ROAD TO
                                            PENRITH

Mosedale....

The Mosedale appearing in the view above is not the
Mosedale mentioned elsewhere in this book and situated
at the foot of Carrock Fell. There are, in fact, six valleys
of this name (signifying *desolation, dreariness*) in Lakeland
and a pastime that might be adopted to fill in a few minutes
while waiting for the rain to stop is to find them all on the
1" Ordnance Survey map of the district (one of them is spelt
Moasdale). If, having done this, it still looks like raining for
ever, make a list of all the different names on the map in
which "thwaite" (a *clearing*) appears : this occupation will
fill in the rest of the day until bedtime. On the 1" Tourist
Map there are 81 *different*, many of them recurring. Enthusiastic
thwaite-spotters will find several others on larger-scale maps.

THE VIEW

SE ← → S

HIGH RAISE 11¾
RAMPSGILL HEAD 11¾
PLACE FELL 8½
HIGH STREET 12½
THORNTHWAITE CRAG
FROSWICK 13¾
ILL BELL 13¾, 12¾
CAUDALE MOOR 12½
HART SIDE 5½
RED SCREES 12½
St SUNDAY CRAG 9⅓
GREAT DODD 4½
CATSTYCAM 7½
HELVELLYN 8
HELVELLYN LOWER MAN 7½

Wolf Crags
White Pike
CLOUGH HEAD 3¼

Threlkeld Common

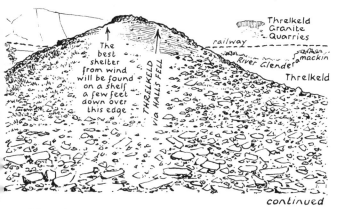

The best shelter from wind will be found on a shelf a few feet down over this edge

THRELKELD VIA HALLS FELL

Threlkeld Granite Quarries
railway
River Glenderamackin
Threlkeld

continued

at Threlkeld....

• Look over both parapets of Threlkeld Bridge. Two streams, the River Glenderamackin and St. John's Beck, at this point unite, passing under the bridge individually but merging as one: the River Greta. The bridge is built over the confluence.
• Walk up the lane signposted Wescoe for 200 yards to the entrance to Riddings, where excellent effigies of a fox and a hound surmount the gateposts. The Blencathra pack was formerly kennelled at Riddings, but is now at Gategill.
• Visit the little glen of Kilnhow Beck. A pleasant path starts near the Horse and Farrier and proceeds upstream to the open fell at Blease Gill with the help of footbridges. This sylvan dell is not publicised and is a charming surprise.

THE VIEW

continued

S · SW

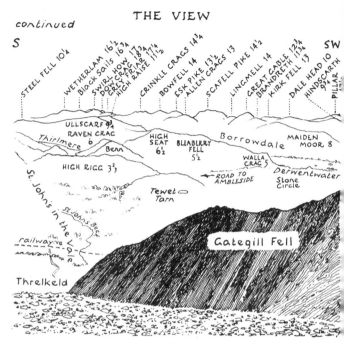

STEEL FELL 10¼ ULLSCARF 9¾ RAVEN CRAC Thirlmere Bern HIGH RIGG 3⅔ St John's in the Vale St John's Beck railway Threlkeld

WETHERLAM 16½ Black Sails 16¾ SWIRL HOW 17¾ DOW CRAG 18¼ GREY FRIAR 17¼ HIGH RAISE 11½ CRINKLE CRAGS 14¾ BOWFELL 14 ESK PIKE 13½ ALLEN CRAGS 13 SCAFELL PIKE 14½ LINGMELL 14 GREAT GABLE 12¾ BRANDRETH 11¾ KIRK FELL 13 DALE HEAD 10 HINDSCARTH 9¾ PILLAR

HIGH SEAT 6½ BLEABERRY FELL 5½ Borrowdale MAIDEN MOOR 8 WALLA CRAG 5 ROAD TO AMBLESIDE Derwentwater Stone Circle Tewet Tarn

Gategill Fell

The White Cross

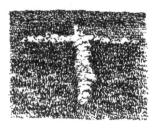

In view from the summit is a landmark that has aroused the curiosity of visitors for a great many years: a collection of white crystallised stones of high quartz content, laid on the grass in the form of a cross on the easy rise to the top of Foule Crag, north of the Saddle.

This cross owes its existence to the industry of Harold Robinson of Threlkeld. Formerly there was a very small cross of stones here (locally ascribed as a memorial to a walker who lost his life on a rough slope adjacent) and Mr. Robinson, an enthusiastic lone hill-wanderer who has climbed his favourite Blencathra hundreds of times, collected more stones (veins of quartzite occur in the native slate nearby) and extended the cross to its present size of 16' by 10' during a succession of visits from 1945 onwards. A much smaller but similar white cross on the southern slope of the Saddle is more recent, and the work of persons unknown.

THE VIEW

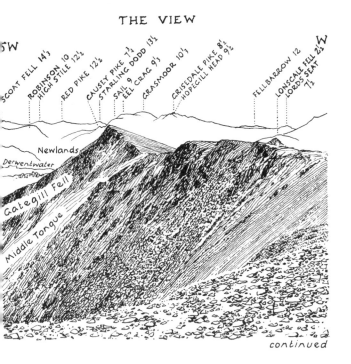

SW

SCOAT FELL 14⅓
ROBINSON 10
HIGH STILE 12½
RED PIKE 12½
CAUSEY PIKE 7¾
STARLING DODD 13½
SAIL 9
EEL CRAG 9⅓
GRASMOOR 10⅓
GRISEDALE PIKE 8½
HOPEGILL HEAD 9½
FELLBARROW 12
LONSCALE FELL 2⅓
LORD'S SEAT 7½

W

Newlands
Derwentwater
Gategill Fell
Middle Tongue

continued

Blencathra's old mines

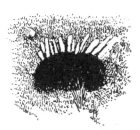

Blencathra has been mined fairly extensively and a variety of ores extracted from workings in the valleys of the Glenderaterra and Glenderamackin and from the adjacent and interlinked Gategill and Woodend mines, the debris of which is still very conspicuous in the Threlkeld landscape. All the mines are now closed, but within living memory were in production and prospering, and finding work for a labour force of 100.

Illustrated is an old level (a little beauty) at the northern workings of the Glenderaterra Mine, leading to a copper vein. The warning must be repeated that disused mine levels are unsafe because of flooding and collapse and often open into vertical pits.

THE VIEW

continued

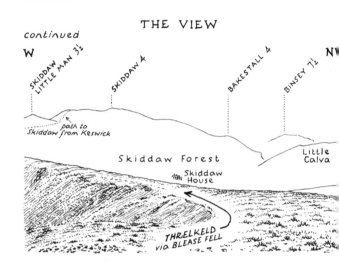

W   NW

SKIDDAW LITTLE MAN 3½

SKIDDAW 4

BAKESTALL 4

BINSEY 7½

path to Skiddaw from Keswick

Little Calva

Skiddaw Forest

Skiddaw House

THRELKELD via BLEASE FELL

RIDGE ROUTE

To SOUTHER FELL, 1680'
2½ miles : E, then NE
Depression at 1355'
350 feet of ascent

Souther Fell is poor fare after Blencathra and the scenery deteriorates all the way. Go along the escarpment to Scales Fell and straight down its eastern slope to the low ridge connecting with Souther Fell, the featureless top of which is reached after a long up-and-down traverse of its grassy ridge.

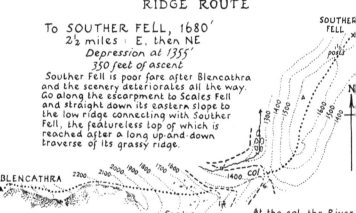

SOUTHER FELL ×

posts

N

BLENCATHRA ▲   2200   2100   2000   1900   1800   1700   1600   1300   1400   1500   1600   1500   1400

1400   col

Scales Fell

HALF A MILE

At the col, the River Glenderamackin is below on the left and Mousthwaite Combe leads on the right to the fields of Scales. There are many tracks hereabouts.

THE VIEW

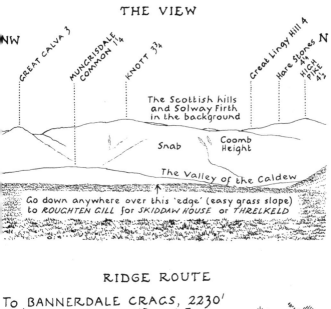

NW

GREAT CALVA 3

MUNGRISDALE COMMON 1¼

KNOTT 3¾

Great Lingy Hill 4

Hare Stones 4¼

HIGH PIKE 4½

N

The Scottish hills and Solway Firth in the background

Snab

Coomb Height

The Valley of the Caldew

Go down anywhere over this 'edge' (easy grass slope) to *ROUGHTEN GILL* for *SKIDDAW HOUSE* or *THRELKELD*

RIDGE ROUTE

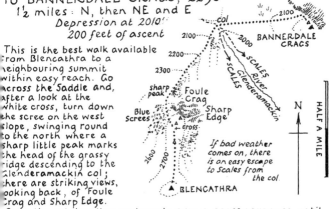

To BANNERDALE CRAGS, 2230'
1½ miles: N, then NE and E
Depression at 2010'
200 feet of ascent

This is the best walk available from Blencathra to a neighbouring summit within easy reach. Go across the Saddle and, after a look at the white cross, turn down the scree on the west slope, swinging round to the north where a sharp little peak marks the head of the grassy ridge descending to the Glenderamackin col; there are striking views, looking back, of Foule Crag and Sharp Edge.

col

2100

2100

BANNERDALE CRAGS

2000

SCALES River

2200

2300

sharp peak

Foule Crag

Blue Screes

Sharp Edge

Glenderamackin

SCALES

cross

2600

2700

If bad weather comes on, there is an easy escape to Scales from the col.

N

HALF A MILE

BLENCATHRA

Cross the col, heading eastwards over a grassy expanse until halted by the edge of Bannerdale Crags, then turn to the right to reach the summit.

Bowfell

2960'

'Bow Fell' (two words)
on Ordnance Survey maps

from Lingmoor Fell

NATURAL FEATURES

A favourite of all fellwalkers, Bowfell is a mountain that commands attention whenever it appears in a view. And more than attention, respect and admiration, too; for it has the rare characteristic of displaying a graceful outline and a sturdy shapeliness on all sides. The fell occupies a splendid position at the hub of three well-known valleys, Great Langdale, Langstrath and Eskdale, rising as a massive pyramid at the head of each, and it is along these valleys that its waters drain, soon assuming the size of rivers. The higher the slopes rise the rougher they become, finally rearing up steeply as a broken rim of rock around the peaked summit and stony top. These crags are of diverse and unusual form, natural curiosities that add an exceptional interest and help to identify Bowfell in the memory. Under the terraced northern precipices, in a dark hollow, is Angle Tarn.

As much as any other mountain, the noble Bowfell may be regarded as affording an entirely typical Lakeland climb, with easy walking over grass giving place to rough scrambling on scree, and a summit deserving of detailed exploration and rewarding visitors with very beautiful views.

Rank Bowfell among the best half-dozen! ※

※The author is not prepared to say, at this stage, which he considers to be the other five. This opinion will be given in the last pages of Book Seven.

• Stonethwaite

▲ GLARAMARA

Wasdale
Head ●

▲ ▲ ESK PIKE

SCAFELL PIKE ▲ BOWFELL
●
Dungeon Ghyll

CRINKLE CRAGS ▲

Boot ●

MILES

0 1 2 3 4 5

MAP

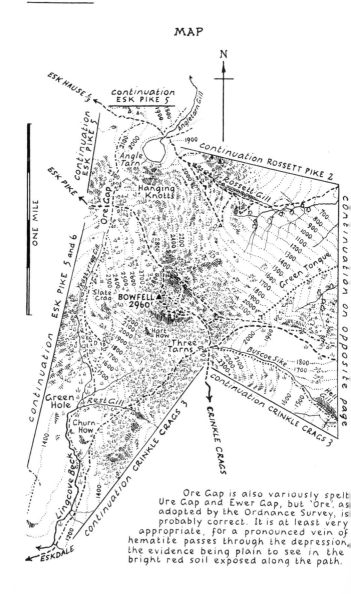

Ore Gap is also variously spelt Ure Gap and Ewer Gap, but 'Ore', as adopted by the Ordnance Survey, is probably correct. It is at least very appropriate, for a pronounced vein of hematite passes through the depression, the evidence being plain to see in the bright red soil exposed along the path.

MAP

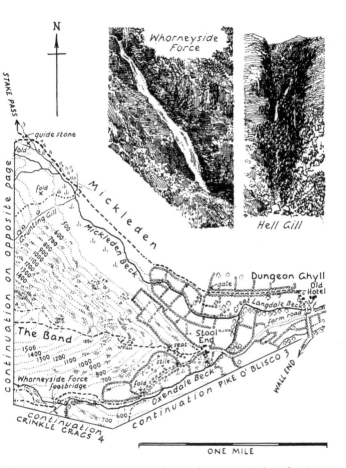

Whorneyside Force

Hell Gill

The county boundary between Cumberland and Westmorland passes over the top of Bowfell, coming up from Wrynose Pass via Crinkle Crags and Three Tarns. From the summit it follows the height of land to Hanging Knotts, where the main ridge is left in favour of the lesser watershed of Rossett Pass, whence it continues the circuit of Mickleden. Thus, Great Langdale and all the waters thereof are wholly within Westmorland.

ASCENT FROM DUNGEON GHYLL
2700 feet of ascent : 3 miles (3¼ via Three Tarns)

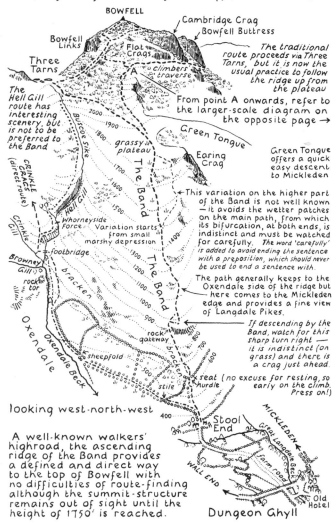

BOWFELL

Cambridge Crag
Bowfell Buttress

Bowfell Links

Flat Crags

Three Tarns

A

climbers traverse

The traditional route proceeds via Three Tarns, but it is now the usual practice to follow the ridge up from the plateau.

The Hell Gill route has interesting scenery, but is not to be preferred to the Band

2000

From point A onwards, refer to the larger-scale diagram on the opposite page →

From point A onwards, refer to the larger-scale diagram on the opposite page →

Green Tongue

1900

1800

grassy plateau

Earing Crag

Green Tongue offers a quick easy descent to Mickleden

Buscoe Sike

The Band

CRINKLE CRAGS (direct route)

1700

1600

1500

Hell Gill

Crinkle Gill

Whorneyside Force

Variation starts from small marshy depression

1400

This variation on the higher part of the Band is not well known — it avoids the wetter patches on the main path, from which its bifurcation, at both ends, is indistinct and must be watched for carefully. The word 'carefully' is added to avoid ending the sentence with a preposition, which should never be used to end a sentence with.

Browney Gill

footbridge

rock tor

bracken

The Band

1300

1200

1100

1000

The path generally keeps to the Oxendale side of the ridge but here comes to the Mickleden edge and provides a fine view of Langdale Pikes

900

bracken

rock gateway

800

Oxendale Beck

sheepfold

Oxendale Beck

700

If descending by the Band, watch for this sharp turn right — it is indistinct (on grass) and there is a crag just ahead.

600

500

stile

hurdle

seat *(no excuse for resting, so early on the climb. Press on!)*

looking west-north-west

400

Stool End

MICKLEDEN

Great Langdale Beck

A well-known walkers' highroad, the ascending ridge of the Band provides a defined and direct way to the top of Bowfell with no difficulties of route-finding although the summit-structure remains out of sight until the height of 1750' is reached.

farm road

WALL END

Old Hotel

Dungeon Ghyll

ASCENT FROM DUNGEON GHYLL

The upper section,
looking west

BB : Bowfell Buttress
CC : Cambridge Crag
FC : Flat Crag

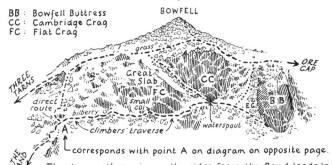

corresponds with point A on diagram on opposite page.

The stony path coming up the ridge from the Band leads to, and is continued as, the climbers' traverse. Ten yards below the point where the horizontal traverse commences the direct route wiggles away up to the left and may be passed unnoticed.

The climbers' traverse is a very enjoyable high-level route leading to excellent rock-scenery. Two recent minor rockfalls have slightly disturbed the path but it is quite distinct and perfectly easy, with a very little very mild scrambling, hardly worth mentioning. The traverse is a series of little ups and downs, but generally keeps to a horizontal course. Except at the small col the ground falls away steeply on the valley side of the path.

The best way off the traverse to the summit lies up the fringe of a 'river' of boulders along the south side of Cambridge Crag, or, more tediously, the wide scree gully between Cambridge Crag and Bowfell Buttress may be ascended. (Cambridge Crag is identifiable, beyond all doubt, by the waterspout gushing from the base of the cliff — and nothing better ever came out of a barrel or a bottle).

The climbers' traverse

The striations of Flat Crags are of particular interest, even to non-geologists. Note how the angle of tilt is repeated in the slope of the Great Slab.

ASCENT FROM WASDALE

Although Bowfell is well hidden from Wasdale Head it is not too distant to be climbed from there in comfortable time, but the walk has the disadvantage (for those who object to re-tracing footsteps) that very little variation of route is possible on the return journey to Wasdale Head. Esk Pike stands in the way and must be climbed first (and traversed later).

For a diagram of the ascent of Esk Pike from Wasdale Head see Esk Pike 8

ASCENT FROM MICKLEDEN
2500 feet of ascent : 1¼ miles from the sheepfold

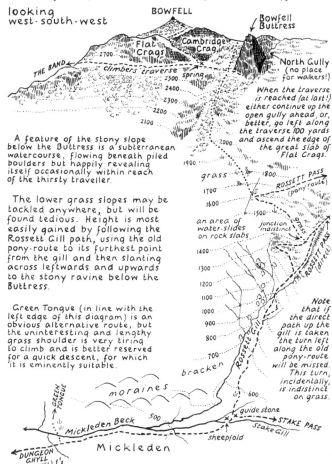

looking
west-south-west

BOWFELL

Bowfell
Buttress

Flat
Crags

Cambridge
Crag.

2700

THE BAND

climbers traverse

2500 spring

2400

2300

2200

2100

North Gully
(no place
for walkers!)

When the traverse
is reached (at last!)
either continue up the
open gully ahead or,
better, go left along
the traverse 100 yards
and ascend the edge of
the great slab of
Flat Crags.

A feature of the stony slope
below the Buttress is a subterranean
watercourse, flowing beneath piled
boulders but happily revealing
itself occasionally within reach
of the thirsty traveller.

2000

1900

grass

1800

1700

1600

ROSSETT PASS
(pony route)

The lower grass slopes may be
tackled anywhere, but will be
found tedious. Height is most
easily gained by following the
Rossett Gill path, using the old
pony-route to its furthest point
from the gill and then slanting
across leftwards and upwards
to the stony ravine below the
Buttress.

1500

junction
indistinct

an area of
water-slides
on rock slabs

grass

ROSSETT PASS (direct)

1400

1300

1200

1100

1000

900

800

Note
that if
the direct
path up the
gill is taken
the turn left
along the old
pony-route
will be missed.
This turn,
incidentally,
is indistinct
on grass.

Green Tongue (in line with the
left edge of this diagram) is an
obvious alternative route, but
the uninteresting and lengthy
grass shoulder is very tiring
to climb and is better reserved
for a quick descent, for which
it is eminently suitable.

700

Rossett Gill

bracken

GREEN TONGUE

moraines

500

600

guide stone

STAKE PASS

Mickleden Beck

Stake Gill

sheepfold

DUNGEON
GHYLL
(OLD HOTEL) 1⅓

Mickleden

The Mickleden face,
2500 feet of continuous ascent, is a route for scramblers
rather than walkers. The rock-scenery becomes imposing
as height is gained, Bowfell Buttress in particular being
an impressive object when seen at close quarters.

ASCENT FROM ESKDALE
2900 feet of ascent : 7½ miles from Boot

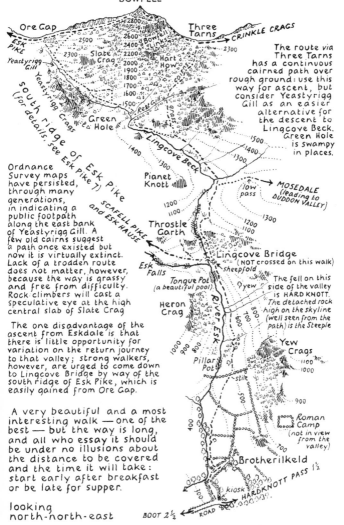

BOWFELL

Ore Gap   Three Tarns   CRINKLE CRAGS

ESK PIKE

Yeastyrigg Gill

Bowfell Links

Slate Crag   Hart How

Green Hole

south ridge of Esk Pike (for details, see Esk Pike 7)

Rest Gill

Lingcove Beck

Planet Knott

SCAFELL PIKE and ESK HAUSE

Throstle Garth

low pass

MOSEDALE (leading to DUDDON VALLEY)

The route via Three Tarns has a continuous cairned path over rough ground: use this way for ascent, but consider Yeastyrigg Gill as an easier alternative for the descent to Lingcove Beck. Green Hole is swampy in places.

Ordnance Survey maps have persisted, through many generations, in indicating a public footpath along the east bank of Yeastyrigg Gill. A few old cairns suggest a path once existed but now it is virtually extinct. Lack of a trodden route does not matter, however, because the way is grassy and free from difficulty. Rock climbers will cast a speculative eye at the high central slab of Slate Crag

The one disadvantage of the ascent from Eskdale is that there is little opportunity for variation on the return journey to that valley; strong walkers, however, are urged to come down to Lingcove Bridge by way of the south ridge of Esk Pike, which is easily gained from Ore Gap.

A very beautiful and a most interesting walk — one of the best — but the way is long, and all who essay it should be under no illusions about the distance to be covered and the time it will take: start early after breakfast or be late for supper.

looking north-north-east

Lingcove Bridge (NOT crossed on this walk)

sheepfold

Esk Falls

Tongue Pot (a beautiful pool)

Heron Crag

River Esk

Pillar Pot

stile

The fell on this side of the valley is HARD KNOTT. The detached rock high on the skyline (well seen from the path) is the Steeple

yew

Yew Crags

Roman Camp (not in view from the valley)

Brotherilkeld

HARDKNOTT PASS 1½

kiosk

BOOT 2½   ROAD

ASCENT FROM STONETHWAITE
2650 feet of ascent : 6½ miles

BOWFELL

ESK PIKE

Ore Gap

Scramblers will note this straight stone-filled gully but are advised against it

Watch closely for a cairned track indistinctly leaving the Esk Hause path, 250 yards beyond Angle Tarn

ROSSETT PIKE

Angle Tarn

ESK HAUSE

GREAT LANGDALE

Tongue Head

grass

The fell here is Allen Crags

Stake Pass

Lining Crag

watersmeet
Bowfell is now in view

Allencrags Gill

Angletarn Gill

The variation to Angle Tarn via the top of Stake Pass has the one advantage of breaking the steepest climbing into two parts, with an easy rising in-between traverse across the broad grassy back of Rossett Pike. There is no such relief on the valley-route from the watersmeet onwards, but the sparkling beck is not so easily forsaken for the dusty zig-zags of the Stake Pass.

× sheepfold

Langstrath Beck

× sheepfold

footbridge
← At this point other pedestrians ascending the valley will depart from it by climbing up to Stake Pass (en route for Great Langdale) and there will be undisturbed solitude for the final two miles of the valley to Angle Tarn, where the broad and busy thoroughfare between Rossett Pass and Esk Hause is joined.

footbridge
Tray Dub
Swan Dub

The fell seen at the valley-head is Esk Pike, not Bowfell.

Dub = a pool in a river

The crag high on the right here is Cam Crag, a shoulder of Glaramara

Blackmoss Pot (look at it)

Blea Rock

High on the left tower Eagle Crag (first) and Sergeant's Crag

Langstrath

It is always interesting to climb a familiar and well-loved mountain by an unfamiliar route, and those walkers who already know Bowfell are recommended to make further acquaintance by approaching this fine hill along beautiful Langstrath.

footbridge
ruin

Greenup Gill

It matters little which side of Langstrath Beck is taken to the foot of Stake Pass. It is usual to cross here, but the older track on the west bank is actually the easier and rather the quicker

Stonethwaite

Before sallying forth reflect that Langstrath means Long Valley, and that Angle Tarn is five miles distant (Ordnance Survey maps prefer the name Long Strath (two words))

Greenup Beck

ROSTHWAITE 1 (road)

looking south-south-west

Cambridge Crag and Bowfell Buttress
from the top of the Great Slab

THE SUMMIT

Bowfell's top is a shattered pyramid, a great heap of stones and boulders and naked rock, a giant cairn in itself.

The rugged summit provides poor picking for the Bowfell sheep, who draw the line at mosses and lichens and look elsewhere for their mountain greenery, and reserves its best rewards for the walkers who climb the natural rocky stairway to its upper limit for here, spread before them for their delectation, is a glorious panorama, which, moreover, may be surveyed and appreciated from positions of repose on the comfortable flat seats of stone (comfortable in the sense that everybody arriving here says how nice it is to sit down) with which the summit is liberally equipped. The leisurely contemplation of the scene will not be assailed by doubts as to whether the highest point has in fact been gained for rough slopes tumble away steeply on all sides.

The top pyramid stands on a sloping plinth which, to the east, extends beyond the base of the pyramid and forms a shelf or terrace where stones are less in evidence. It is from this shelf that Bowfell's main crags fall away, and from which, with care, they may be viewed; care is necessary because the boulders to be negotiated in carrying out this inspection are in a state of balance, in places, and liable to heel over and trap a leg.

It is possible, and does happen, that walkers ascend Bowfell and traverse its top quite unaware of the imposing line of crags overlooking Mickleden: from the summit and the shelf-track there is little to indicate the presence of steep cliffs. But to miss seeing the crags is to miss seeing half the glory of Bowfell.

THE SUMMIT

continued

KEY:

NG : North Gully
BB : Bowfell Buttress
EG : Easy Gully (scree)
CC : Cambridge Crag
WS : Waterspout
RB : River of Boulders
FC : Flat Crags
GS : do Great Slab
CT : Climbers' Traverse
WR : Walkers' Route to avoid Traverse
BL : Bowfell Links
▲ Summit

	for ROCK CLIMBERS	for WALKERS
NG	✓	-
BB	✓	-
EG	✓	-
CC	✓	-
WS	✓✓	✓✓
RB	✓	-
FC	✓	-
GS		
CT	✓	-
WR		✓
BL	✓	-
▲		✓✓

PLAN OF THE SUMMIT

YARDS
0   100   200

DESCENTS : The sloping grass shelf, east of the actual summit, carries the only path across the top: it links Ore Gap with Three Tarns. Two well-scratched tracks go down from the cairn and join this path : one, on the south, descends first in line with Three Tarns but is turned leftwards by the uncompromising rim of Bowfell Links; the other, shorter, goes down north inclining north-east with many simple variations among the boulders. For Langdale the steep lower section of the Three Tarns path may be avoided by using a terrace on the left at a gap in the wall of rocks (WR on the plan above). Direct descents to Eskdale over the steepening boulder slopes are not feasible.

In mist, the only safe objectives are Ore Gap (for Wasdale, Borrowdale or Eskdale) and Three Tarns (for Langdale via the Band, or Eskdale) avoiding Bowfell Links on the way thereto.

The Great Slab of Flat Crags

RIDGE ROUTES

To CRINKLE CRAGS, 2816′ : 1½ miles
SE, E, SE and then generally S
Main depression (Three Tarns) at 2320′
600 feet of ascent

A rough ridge-walk of high quality

A bee-line for Three Tarns runs foul of Bowfell Links, and the summit notes should be consulted for getting down to the gap. From there onwards the gradual climb to Crinkle Crags, with its many turns and twists and ups and downs is entirely delightful, *but not in mist.* (See Crinkle Crags 13)

Shelter Crags   summit   Long Top

GREAT LANGDALE ←   → ESKDALE

Crinkle Crags, as seen on the descent to Three Tarns from the summit of Bowfell.   The path is indicated. The first three Crinkles are hidden behind Shelter Crags.

To ESK PIKE, 2903′ : 1 mile
NW, W and NW
Depression (Ore Gap) at 2575′
340 feet of ascent

A straightforward, rather rough, walk

The path going up Esk Pike from Ore Gap is visible from afar, but the way thereto across Bowfell's stony top is less clearly marked but well indicated by cairns. Turn aside to look down the wide gully south of Bowfell Buttress ; the more impressive north gully may also be reached by a short and easy detour.

BOWFELL

Flat Crags

Bowfell Links

Three Tarns

Shelter Crags

CRINKLE CRAGS

N

ONE MILE

ESK PIKE

Hanging Knotts

Ore Gap

top north gully

top south gully

BOWFELL

*Three views
    from the Band*

Right:
  Browney Gill and Cold Pike

Bottom Right:
  Pike o' Blisco

Below:
  Pike o' Stickle

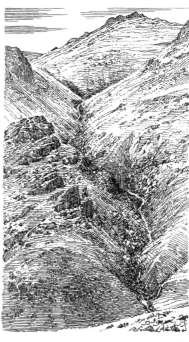

THE VIEW

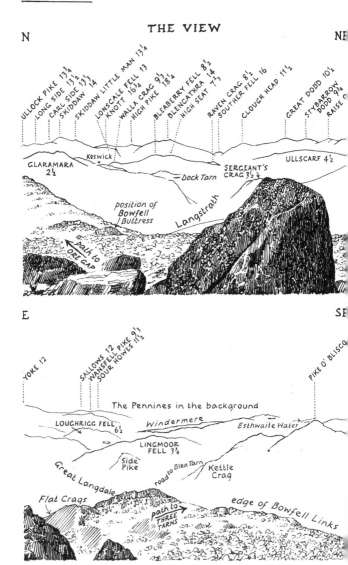

THE VIEW

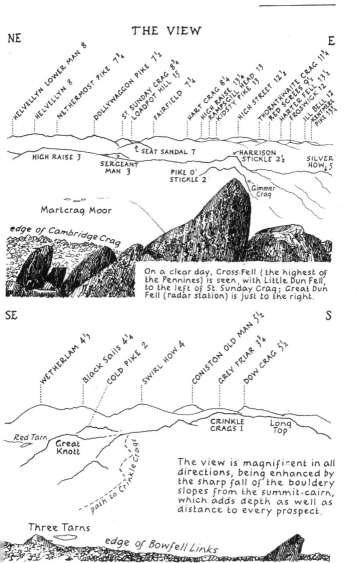

NE

HELVELLYN LOWER MAN 8
HELVELLYN 8
NETHERMOST PIKE 7¾
DOLLYWAGGON PIKE 7½
ST. SUNDAY CRAG 8¾
LOADPOT HILL 15
FAIRFIELD 7¾
HART CRAG 8¼
HIGH RAISE 13¼
RAMPSGILL HEAD 13
KIDSTY PIKE 13
HIGH STREET 12½
THORNTHWAITE CRAG 11¼
RED SCREES 9½
HARTER FELL 13½
FROSWICK 12
ILL BELL 12
KENTMERE PIKE 13¾

E

HIGH RAISE 3
SEAT SANDAL 7
SERGEANT MAN 3
HARRISON STICKLE 2½
SILVER HOW 5

PIKE O' STICKLE 2

Gimmer Crag

Martcrag Moor

edge of Cambridge Crag

On a clear day, Cross Fell (the highest of the Pennines) is seen, with Little Dun Fell, to the left of St. Sunday Crag; Great Dun Fell (radar station) is just to the right.

SE

WETHERLAM 4½
Black Sails 4¼
COLD PIKE 2
SWIRL HOW 4
CONISTON OLD MAN 5½
GREY FRIAR 3¾
DOW CRAG 5½

S

Red Tarn
Great Knott
CRINKLE CRAGS 1
Long Top

path to Crinkle Crags

The view is magnificent in all directions, being enhanced by the sharp fall of the bouldery slopes from the summit cairn, which adds depth as well as distance to every prospect.

Three Tarns

edge of Bowfell Links

THE VIEW

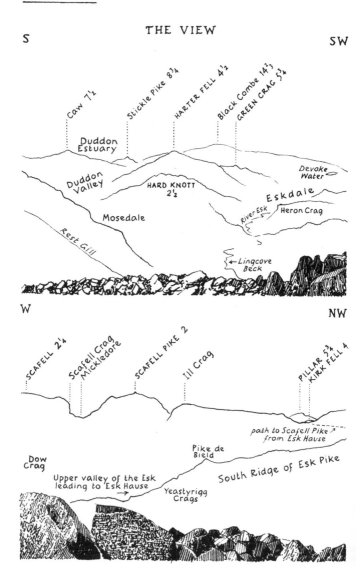

S

SW

Caw 7½

Stickle Pike 8¾

HARTER FELL 4½

Black Combe 14¾

GREEN CRAG 5¾

Duddon
Estuary

Duddon
Valley

HARD KNOTT
2½

Mosedale

Rest Gill

Devoke
Water

Eskdale

River Esk

Heron Crag

← Lingcove
Beck

W

NW

SCAFELL 2¼

Scafell Crag
Mickledore

SCAFELL PIKE 2

Ill Crag

PILLAR 5¾

KIRK FELL 4

path to Scafell Pike →
from Esk Hause

Dow
Crag

Pike de
Bield

South Ridge of Esk Pike

Upper valley of the Esk
leading to Esk Hause →

Yeastyrigg
Crags

THE VIEW

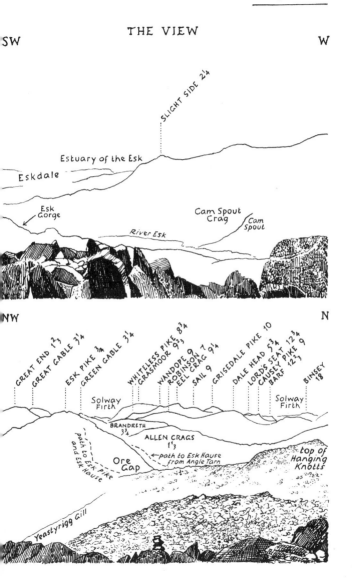

SW

W

SLIGHT SIDE 2¼

Estuary of the Esk

Eskdale

Esk Gorge

Cam Spout Crag

Cam Spout

River Esk

NW

N

GREAT END 12¾
GREAT GABLE 3¾
ESK PIKE 3¾
GREEN GABLE 3¾
WHITELESS PIKE 8¾
GRASMOOR 9¾
WANDOPE 9
ROBINSON 7
EEL CRAG 9¼
SAIL 9
GRISEDALE PIKE 10
DALE HEAD 5¾
LORD'S SEAT 12¾
CAUSEY PIKE 9
BARF 12¾
BINSEY 18

Solway Firth

Solway Firth

BRANDRETH 3¾

ALLEN CRAGS 1¾

path to Esk Pike and Esk Hause

← path to Esk Hause from Angle Tarn

Ore Gap

top of Hanging Knotts

Yeastyrigg Gill

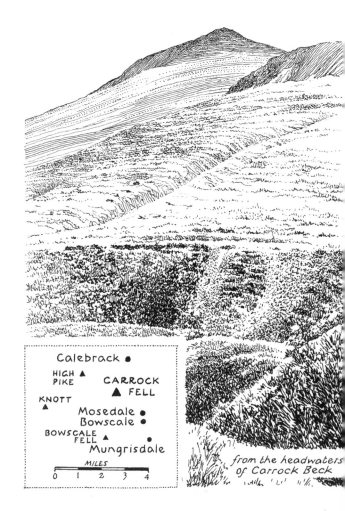

Calebrack ●

HIGH ▲
PIKE   CARROCK
            ▲ FELL

KNOTT
▲
        Mosedale ●
        Bowscale ●
BOWSCALE
FELL ▲ Mungrisdale ●

MILES
0   1   2   3   4

from the headwaters of Carrock Beck

NATURAL FEATURES

Carrock Fell caters for a wide variety of interests. More than any other fell in the district it attracts people who are not regular walkers or climbers—people, indeed, to whom walking for its own sake has little appeal and is here, on Carrock, only a means to an end and not an end in itself. This rough little height is, first and foremost, a very rich geological field, for here the extensive area of Skiddaw slates and shales, the basic foundation of practically the whole of the Northern Fells, abruptly terminates against a rugged upthrust of igneous or volcanic rocks of different series dovetailed in such a way as to provide an absorbing study for the geologist, while the bed of the Caldew at the western base is notable as one of the few places where the underlying creamy-pink Skiddaw granite is exposed. One need have no special knowledge to see at a glance that Carrock Fell is different from its neighbours: appearance alone is enough, the bouldery slopes contrasting sharply with those of smooth grass all around. Carrock Fell is something of a rebel, a nonconformist, the odd man out— it would look more at home at the head of Borrowdale or Langdale amongst others of like kind.

In the field of mining Carrock is a famous name, having a series of veins that have yielded a variety of rich and rare metals and other minerals. Carrock Mine is especially well known for its supplies of wolfram. Although not now being worked the area is often visited by mineralogists.

Other fells have interesting rocks and minerals also—but Carrock has more than natural attractions on display. Its summit is unique, being ringed by the collapsed walls of an ancient hill-fort of unknown age and origin, thought to be early British, which must, in its time, have been a remarkable stronghold. This in itself is enough to excite the many archaeologists and antiquaries who, individually and in groups, make pilgrimages to the place, but the east base of the fell, too, has scores of artificial mounds that might upon investigation reveal something of the story of Carrock B.C.

continued

Carrock Fell, from the shooting-box on Great Lingy Hill

NATURAL FEATURES
continued

Amongst the igneous rocks of which the fell is formed is gabbro — the stuff the Black Coolin of Skye are made of but a rarity in Lakeland. It is in evidence in the crags of the eastern escarpment and on the boulder-strewn slopes below. Gabbro is an ideal rock for climbing, and here is the one and only climbing-ground in the Northern Fells — very handily situated just above an unenclosed road (the one going *north* out of Mosedale) where cars may be parked. The eastern face of the fell, in fact, everywhere presents attractive scenery.

The heaps of piled boulders on the fell, both on the south and east fronts, provide several safe borrans for foxes in their crevices, these refuges being well-known to followers of the Blencathra pack. When a fox is run to earth on Carrock the hunt is often called off and the frustrated pursuers retire brushless. Cheers for Carrock, therefore, on humane grounds also.

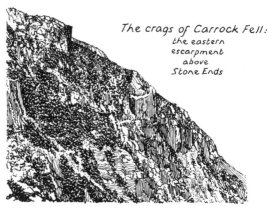

The crags of Carrock Fell:
the eastern
escarpment
above
Stone Ends

Geologists, mineralogists, archaeologists, rock-climbers and foxes : all these are provided for. What is there for the ordinary walker, who simply ascends hills because he likes doing it ? Well, Carrock is a delightful climb, as rough as one cares to make it. In the northern area of Lakeland it ranks next to Blencathra for interest and excitement and beauty of surroundings; in season it has its own special reward for bilberry addicts: there are acres to graze upon. Let others tap rocks with hammers, and dig holes, and prospect with pans, and scale precipices if they wish; heaven for the walker with no special scholarship is at hand in the lush green pastures around the summit. But visit the cairn, of course, for yet another of Carrock's manifold attractions is its glorious view.

Carrock Mine

Carrock Mine is situated at the confluence of Grainsgill Beck and Brandy Gill, in a side-valley of the Caldew. It has been a productive source of mineral wealth in variety, but is best known for its output of the heavy metal *tungsten* (*wolfram*), a rare mineral not found elsewhere in Lakeland. The mine closed a few decades ago, not due to exhaustion of supplies but because of a fall in world prices — therefore its re-opening is a future possibility, although clearly any speculator will be faced with a big capital expenditure, the buildings having decayed beyond repair.

Mineral veins occur in fractures of the rock, commonly following straight courses of varying depth, with branches, and it is usual to find veins running parallel to each other. Carrock Mine offers a good illustration of this. Standing at the head of the artificial 'cut' on the eastern shoulder of Coomb Height one can look directly down its length to Grainsgill Beck and see the line continuing up the opposite slope in a series of levels and shafts — a perfectly straight line over a distance of half a mile. Similarly, on the east side of Brandy Gill another vein is noticeable parallel to the first. The spoil-heaps of mica-quartz are almost white and very conspicuous.

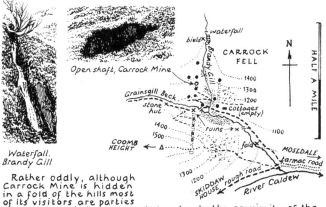

Open shaft, Carrock Mine

Waterfall. Brandy Gill

Rather oddly, although Carrock Mine is hidden in a fold of the hills most of its visitors are parties of motorists, their presence being due to the proximity of the mine to the terminus of the surfaced road along the Caldew valley, which is becoming increasingly popular as a Sunday afternoon picnic-place. These visitors are not shod for scrambling over rough ground and often have children and dogs with them: the warning must be repeated that *disused mine-workings are dangerous*, Carrock Mine in fact having some unfenced open shafts. Inspection at a distance is safe; exploration is hazardous.

A source of valuable information on the geology and mineralogy of Lakeland is provided by a book now out of print but still obtainable through public libraries: MINES AND MINING IN THE LAKE DISTRICT by John Postlethwaite (published 1877; second edition 1889; third 1913).

MAP

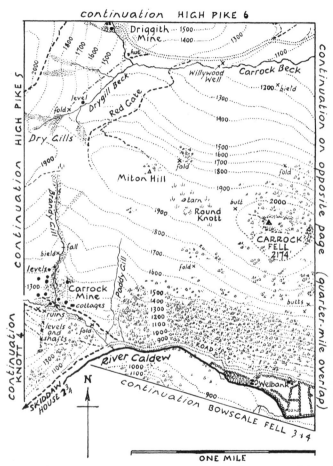

continuation HIGH PIKE 6

continuation HIGH PIKE 5

continuation on opposite page (quarter-mile overlap)

continuation KNOTT 4

continuation BOWSCALE FELL 3+4

Driggith Mine

hut

Willywood Well

Carrock Beck

field

level

fold

Drygill Beck

Red Gate

Dry Gills

fold

Miton Hill

tarn

Round Knott

butt

CARROCK FELL 2174

field

fall

levels

Carrock Mine

cottages

Paddy Gill

Brandy Gill

fold

ruins

levels and shafts

fold

butts

ROAD

River Caldew

Welbank

SKIDDAW HOUSE 2¾

N

ONE MILE

Mosedale means dreary valley, but the name is inappropriate to the mile of emerald pastures watered by the Caldew between the hamlet and Welbank — a charming example of the result of many centuries of patient husbandry, and a typical Lakeland scene.

MAP

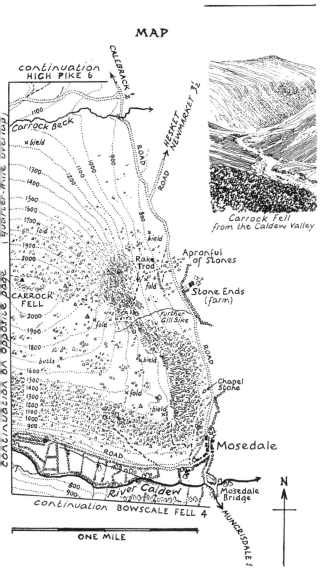

continuation
HIGH PIKE 6

CALEBRACK 2

Carrock Beck

× bield

HESKET NEWMARKET 3½

ROAD

ROAD

1100
1300
1400
1500
1600
1700
1900
2000

1000
900
800

× bield

Rake Trod

fold

Apronful of Stones

Stone Ends (farm)

CARROCK FELL

2000
1900
1800
1600
1500
1400
1300
1200
1100
1000
900

fold

fold

butts ×

Further Gill Sike

× bield

ROAD

Chapel Stone

× bield

fold

Mosedale

800
900

River Caldew

Mosedale Bridge

N

continuation BOWSCALE FELL 4

MUNGRISDALE 1

ONE MILE

(quarter-mile overlap)

CONTINUATION ON OPPOSITE PAGE

Carrock Fell
from the Caldew valley

ASCENT FROM MOSEDALE
1450 feet of ascent : 2 miles

• Carrock Fe[ll]
should not b[e]
climbed in mis[t]

The descent of the fe[ll]
to Mosedale will b[e]
found troublesom[e]
if neither rout[e]
can be locate[d]
Memorise th[e]
details o[f]
the wa[y]
up!

A necklace of stones
— the fallen ramparts
of an ancient Hill Fort

CARROCK FELL
tumulus east peak

sheepfold

1900 2000
1900
heather
1800

two short walls
(bields)

plateau
a strange landscape
of scattered blocks and
boulders in heather

1700
1600
1500

no beaten track
but a natural path
suggests itself

good sheepfold
against crag

pool
edge of
plateau 1400

△ cairn

× bield

conspicuous tree (a usefu[l]
landmark for
finding the path
when descendin[g]

1500
scree rake
path
obliterated
by scree

bield ×

1300
1200
× bield
gorse and
scree
crag 1100

1000

green path
on shelf

Leave road
at corner of
wall (no path
at first)

sheep △ bracken
tracks
900
800

gorse

STONE[Y]
ENDS
ROAD

← CARROCK MINE 2

ROAD

River Caldew

Mosedal[e]

looking
north-west

Mosedale Bridge
(old and new[)]

Two paths are shown,
and the help of one or the other
is necessary to negotiate safely
the barrier of boulders on the
steep initial slope. The paths,
neither of them cairned nor
continuously distinct, come to an end
when the broad heathery plateau is reached
— progress is then easy and gradients gentle.

↓ MUNGRISDALE 1

Carrock Fell has quite exceptional
interest for the geologist, the mineralogist and
the antiquary, and even the unlearned fellwalker
will find the ascent out of the ordinary.

ASCENT FROM STONE ENDS
1400 feet of ascent : 1¼ miles

looking west

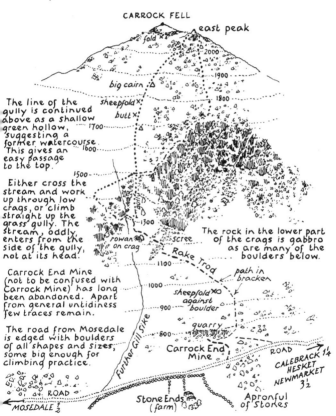

CARROCK FELL

east peak

fold

2000

big cairn

1900

sheepfold

1800

butt

1700

1600

1500

1300

rowan on crag

scree

Rake Trod

path in bracken

1100

1000

sheepfold against boulder

900

quarry

800

Carrock End Mine

ROAD

CALEBRACK 1¼
HESKET
NEWMARKET 3½

Further Gill Sike

ROAD

MOSEDALE ½

Stone Ends (farm)

Apronful of Stones

The line of the gully is continued above as a shallow green hollow, suggesting a former watercourse. This gives an easy passage to the top.

Either cross the stream and work up through low crags, or climb straight up the grass gully. The stream, oddly, enters from the side of the gully, not at its head.

Carrock End Mine (not to be confused with Carrock Mine) has long been abandoned. Apart from general untidiness few traces remain.

The road from Mosedale is edged with boulders of all shapes and sizes, some big enough for climbing practice.

The rock in the lower part of the crags is gabbro as are many of the boulders below.

This is the shortest way to the top from a motor road, and the most straightforward. It affords intimate views of the crags, passing through them by a simple grass gully.   This route, 'Rake Trod', is the one used and recommended by local people.

ASCENT FROM CALEBRACK
1300 feet of ascent : 3½ miles

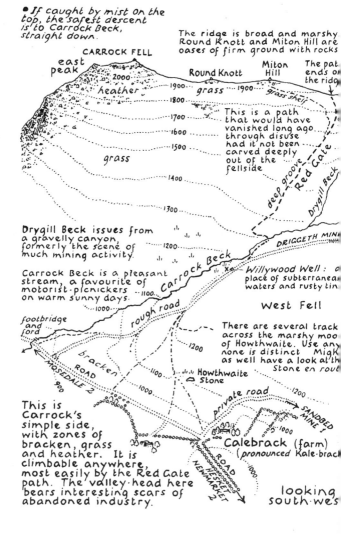

● If caught by mist on the top, the safest descent is to Carrock Beck, straight down.

The ridge is broad and marshy. Round Knott and Miton Hill are oases of firm ground with rocks

CARROCK FELL

Round Knott

Miton Hill

The pat ends on the ridg

east peak

2000

heather

grass

1900

1900

grass shel

1800

1700

This is a path that would have vanished long ago through disuse had it not been carved deeply out of the fellside

1600

1500

grass

deep groove

Red Gate

1400

Drygill Beck

1300

Drygill Beck issues from a gravelly canyon, formerly the scene of much mining activity.

1200

Carrock Beck

DRIGGETH MIN

Carrock Beck is a pleasant stream, a favourite of motorist-picnickers on warm sunny days.

1100

Willywood Well : a place of subterranean waters and rusty tin

1000

West Fell

footbridge and ford

rough road

There are several track across the marshy moo of Howthwaite. Use an none is distinct Migh as well have a look at th Stone en rout

bracken

MOSEDALE 2

ROAD

1200

900

1100

Howthwaite Stone

1000

private road

1200

1000

This is Carrock's simple side, with zones of bracken, grass and heather. It is climbable anywhere, most easily by the Red Gate path. The valley-head here bears interesting scars of abandoned industry.

SANDBED MINE 1

Calebrack (farm) (pronounced Kale-brack)

ROAD HESKET NEWMARKET 2

looking south-wes

THE SUMMIT

The top of the fell is elliptical in plan, with a cairn on low rocks at each extremity. Draped like a necklace around the western top (the higher) is a broad band of stones, the ruined wall of the ancient fort: a continuous link except for four breaches corresponding to the main points of the compass and serving as gateways. Within this wall is a heap of stones, possibly a tumulus, now hollowed out as a shelter. There is no obvious trace of buildings, and visitors should not be deceived by an enclosure on the south side, this being only a sheepfold built from the stones of the wall. New bilberry shoots impart a bright sheen to the top in early summer.

best fragment of
original masonry

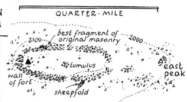

N

QUARTER-MILE

best fragment of
original masonry
2100   2000
tumulus
wall
of fort   east
peak
sheepfold

PLAN OF SUMMIT

The collapsed walls of
the fort, at the
south gateway

continued

THE SUMMIT

continued

DESCENTS. Descent on the east and south flanks is tricky, the few breaches in the impassable slope of crags and boulders at the edge of the plateau being difficult to locate, even in clear weather. The simplest plan is to follow the natural fall of land to the dry gully into which Further Gill Sike enters on the right and go down to Stone Ends by way of Rake Trod. A route to Mosedale direct may be attempted if it has been used observantly for the ascent.

In mist, the safest plan is to go down the easy north slope to Carrock Beck and follow the stream to the road.

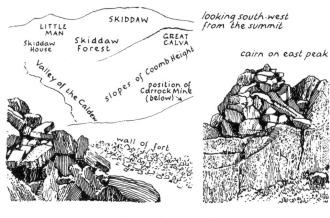

looking south-west from the summit

cairn on east peak

RIDGE ROUTE

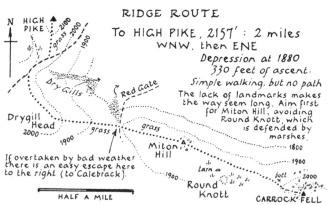

To HIGH PIKE, 2157': 2 miles
WNW, then ENE

Depression at 1880
330 feet of ascent.

Simple walking, but no path

The lack of landmarks makes the way seem long. Aim first for Miton Hill, avoiding Round Knott, which is defended by marshes.

If overtaken by bad weather there is an easy escape here to the right (to Calebrack).

HALF A MILE

THE VIEW

The best section of the view is eastwards, not towards Lakeland but away from it, across the wide and fertile valley of the Eden to the Pennines beyond: an extensive yet detailed scene better observed from the east peak.
The neighbouring heights do not show to advantage, but there is a good prospect of the fells around Ullswater, and Great Gable, Pillar & Co. fill in the notch of the Glenderaterra valley quite neatly. The upper Caldew valley features well.
The Solway Firth appears in the north-west, with Criffell prominent just to the right of the summit of High Pike.

Principal Fells

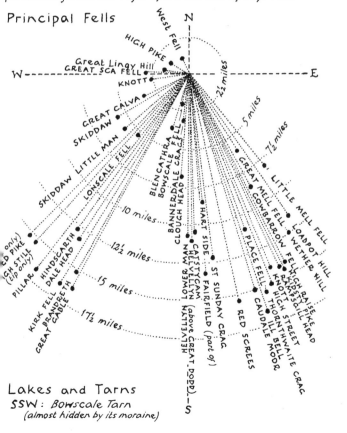

Lakes and Tarns
SSW: *Bowscale Tarn*
(almost hidden by its moraine)

Crinkle Crags 2816'

from Pike o' Blisco

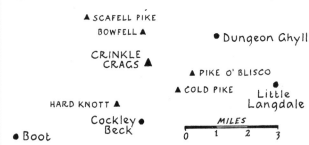

▲ SCAFELL PIKE
BOWFELL ▲
● Dungeon Ghyll

CRINKLE
CRAGS ▲

▲ PIKE O' BLISCO

▲ COLD PIKE
Little ●
Langdale

HARD KNOTT ▲
Cockley ●
Beck

● Boot

MILES
0   1   2   3

NATURAL FEATURES

Some mountains are obviously named by reference to their physical characteristics. Crinkle Crags is one of these, and it was probably first so called by the dalesfolk of the valleys to the east and around the head of Windermere, whence its lofty serrated ridge, a succession of knobs and depressions, is aptly described by the name. These undulations, seeming trivial from a distance, are revealed at close range as steep buttresses and gullies above wild declivities, a scene of desolation and rugged grandeur equalled by few others in the district. Nor is the Eskdale flank any gentler, for here too are gaunt shattered crags rising from incredibly rough slopes. The high pass of Three Tarns links the ridge with Bowfell to the north while southwards Wrynose Bottom is the boundary.

Crinkle Crags is much too good to be missed. For the mountaineer who prefers his mountains rough, who likes to see steep craggy slopes towering before him into the sky, who enjoys an up-and-down ridge walk full of interesting nooks and corners, who has an appreciative eye for magnificent views, this is a climb deserving of high priority. But it is not a place to visit in bad weather for the top is confusing, with ins and outs as well as ups and downs and a sketchy path that cannot be relied on. Crinkle Crags merits respect, and should be treated with respect; then it will yield the climber a mountain walk long to be remembered with pleasure.

Is it 'Crinkle Crags IS ...' or 'Crinkle Crags ARE ...' ?
Is it 'Three Tarns IS ....' or 'Three Tarns ARE ...' ?
IS sounds right but looks wrong!

The outline of Crinkle Crags from Great Langdale

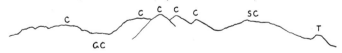

C : The five Crinkles   GC : Great Cove
T : Rock tower near Three Tarns   SC : Shelter Crags

The highest Crinkle (2816') is second from the left on the diagram. When seen from the valley it does not appear to be the highest, as it is set back a little from the line of the others.

Crinkle Crags 3

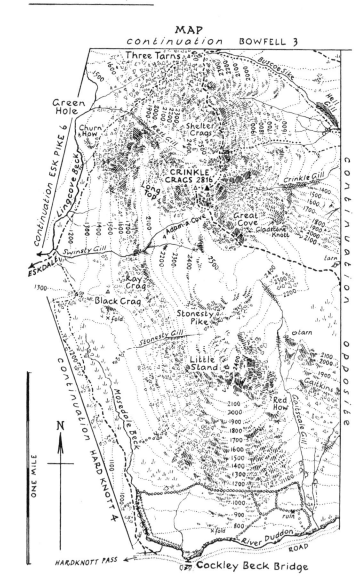

MAP

continuation BOWFELL 4

The Band

Dry Gill

1400
1300
1200
1100

Whorneyside Force

footbridge

seat

Stool End

DUNGEON GHYLL ½

fold

Oxendale Beck

900
800
700

500

600
700
800
900
1000
1100
1200
1400
1500

Isaac Gill

Brown How

continuation PIKE O' BLISCO 3

N

Great Knott

Browney Gill

1800
1700
2000
1900
2100

Red Tarn

COLD PIKE

1800

continuation PIKE O' BLISCO 3

1700

fold

1900
1800
1700
1600
1500
1400

Rough Crags

LITTLE LANGDALE

Three Shire Stone
summit

Wrynose Pass

1300
1200
1100
1000
900

Wrynose Breast

ROAD

River Duddon

Wrynose Bottom

A strange outcrop of striated rocks in Adam-a-Cove

Crinkle Crags has no stone walls, other than those of the intakes above the River Duddon, which are really valley-walls, and in this respect it is typical of the neighbouring Bowfell and Scafell groups, which do not carry the long walls so characteristic of the fells in the eastern part of the district.

ONE MILE

On this map, only regularly-used paths are shown. Other routes are suggested, with qualifications, on the diagrams of ascents.

ASCENT FROM DUNGEON GHYLL (via RED TARN)
2600 feet of ascent : 4 miles

As far as Red Tarn, the route is that used for the ascent of Pike o' Blisco (the craggy slopes of which tower up on the left throughout) and for the high-level walk to Wrynose Pass.

CRINKLE CRAGS

COLD PIKE

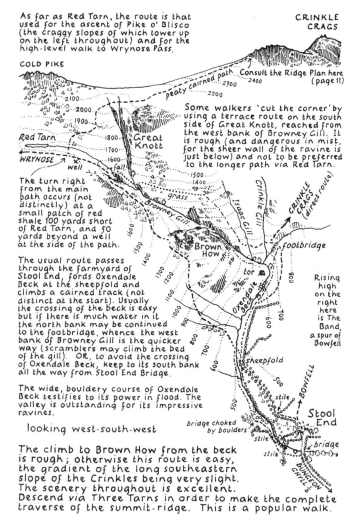

Consult the Ridge Plan here (page 11)

Some walkers 'cut the corner' by using a terrace route on the south side of Great Knott, reached from the west bank of Browney Gill. It is rough (and dangerous in mist, for the sheer wall of the ravine is just below) and not to be preferred to the longer path via Red Tarn.

The turn right from the main path occurs (not distinctly) at a small patch of red shale 100 yards short of Red Tarn, and 50 yards beyond a well at the side of the path.

The usual route passes through the farmyard of Stool End, fords Oxendale Beck at the sheepfold and climbs a cairned track (not distinct at the start). Usually the crossing of the beck is easy but if there is much water in it the north bank may be continued to the footbridge, whence the west bank of Browney Gill is the quicker way (scramblers may climb the bed of the gill). OR, to avoid the crossing of Oxendale Beck, keep to its south bank all the way from Stool End Bridge.

The wide, bouldery course of Oxendale Beck testifies to its power in flood. The valley is outstanding for its impressive ravines.

looking west-south-west

Rising high on the right here is The Band, a spur of Bowfell.

The climb to Brown How from the beck is rough; otherwise this route is easy, the gradient of the long southeastern slope of the Crinkles being very slight. The scenery throughout is excellent. Descend via Three Tarns in order to make the complete traverse of the summit-ridge. This is a popular walk.

ASCENT FROM DUNGEON GHYLL (*via* THREE TARNS)
2650 feet of ascent : 4 miles

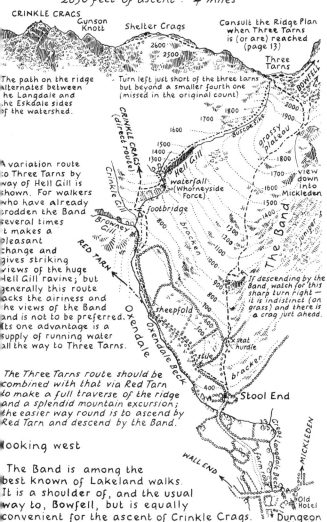

CRINKLE CRAGS
Gunson Knott
Shelter Crags

Consult the Ridge Plan when Three Tarns is (or are) reached (page 13)

2600
2500

Three Tarns

BOWFELL

The path on the ridge alternates between the Langdale and the Eskdale sides of the watershed.

Turn left just short of the three tarns but beyond a smaller fourth one (missed in the original count)

CRINKLE CRAGS (direct route)

2000
1900

1800
1700
1600

Buscoe Sike

grassy plateau

A variation route to Three Tarns by way of Hell Gill is shown. For walkers who have already trodden the Band several times it makes a pleasant change and gives striking views of the huge Hell Gill ravine; but generally this route lacks the airiness and the views of the Band and is not to be preferred. Its one advantage is a supply of running water all the way to Three Tarns.

1500
1400
1300

Hell Gill

Crinkle Gill

Browney Gill

RED TARN

waterfall (Whorneyside Force)

footbridge

800

bracken

1800

1700
1600
1500
1400
1300
1200
1100

view down into Mickleden

The Band

juniper

If descending by the Band, watch for this sharp turn right — it is indistinct (on grass) and there is a crag just ahead.

Oxendale Beck

sheepfold

1000

900

800

700

600

500

x seat hurdle

stile

bracken

The Three Tarns route should be combined with that via Red Tarn to make a full traverse of the ridge and a splendid mountain excursion; the easier way round is to ascend by Red Tarn and descend by the Band.

400

Stool End

looking west

Great Langdale Beck

farm road

MICKLEDEN

The Band is among the best known of Lakeland walks. It is a shoulder of, and the usual way to, Bowfell, but is equally convenient for the ascent of Crinkle Crags.

WALL END

Old Hotel

Dungeon Ghyll

ASCENT FROM DUNGEON GHYLL
(DIRECT CLIMB FROM OXENDALE)
2550 feet of ascent : 3½ miles

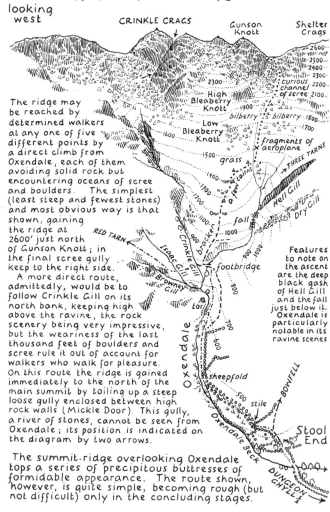

looking west

CRINKLE CRAGS

Gunson Knott

Shelter Crags

2600
2500
2400
2300
curious channel of scree 2200
2100

2300

High Bleaberry Knott

1900

bilberry   bilberry   1800

Low Bleaberry Knott

1700

fragments of aeroplane

1600

THREE TARNS

grass

1500

few cairns

1400

Hell Gill

1300

1700

fall

Dry Gill

1000

RED TARN

900

bracken

1000

Isaac Gill

Crinkle Gill

footbridge

800

Browney Gill

tor

Oxendale

700

600

500

sheepfold

BOWFELL

stile

Oxendale Beck

Stool End

DUNGEON GHYLL

The ridge may be reached by determined walkers at any one of five different points by a direct climb from Oxendale, each of them avoiding solid rock but encountering oceans of scree and boulders. The simplest (least steep and fewest stones) and most obvious way is that shown, gaining the ridge at 2600' just north of Gunson Knott; in the final scree gully keep to the right side.

A more direct route, admittedly, would be to follow Crinkle Gill on its north bank, keeping high above the ravine, the rock scenery being very impressive, but the weariness of the last thousand feet of boulders and scree rule it out of account for walkers who walk for pleasure. On this route the ridge is gained immediately to the north of the main summit by toiling up a steep loose gully enclosed between high rock walls (Mickle Door). This gully, a river of stones, cannot be seen from Oxendale; its position is indicated on the diagram by two arrows.

Features to note on the ascent are the deep black gash of Hell Gill and the fall just below it. Oxendale is particularly notable in its ravine scenes

The summit-ridge overlooking Oxendale tops a series of precipitous buttresses of formidable appearance. The route shown, however, is quite simple, becoming rough (but not difficult) only in the concluding stages.

ASCENT FROM ESKDALE
2650 feet of ascent : 7½ miles from Boot
(8 miles via Three Tarns)

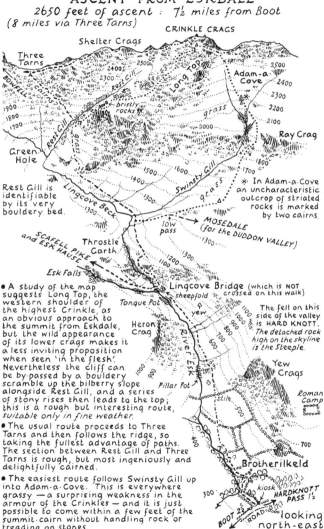

CRINKLE CRAGS

Shelter Crags

Three Tarns

2400 2500

2300

Rest Gill

Long Top

spring

Adam-a-Cove

2500

2400

2300

2200

2100

bristly rocks

grass

2000

Ray Crag

1800

1900

1800

1700

Green Hole

Rest Gill

grass

1400

1500

1600

Swinsty Gill

1700

1700

※ In Adam-a-Cove an uncharacteristic outcrop of striated rocks is marked by two cairns.

Rest Gill is identifiable by its very bouldery bed.

Lingcove Beck

1300

1300

grass

low pass

MOSEDALE (for the DUDDON VALLEY)

1300

SCAFELL PIKE and ESK HAUSE

Throstle Garth

1300

1200

1100

Esk Falls

Lingcove Bridge (which is NOT crossed on this walk)

sheepfold

yew

The fell on this side of the valley is HARD KNOTT. The detached rock high on the skyline is the Steeple.

● A study of the map suggests Long Top, the western shoulder of the highest Crinkle, as an obvious approach to the summit from Eskdale, but the wild appearance of its lower crags makes it a less inviting proposition when seen 'in the flesh'. Nevertheless the cliff can be by-passed by a bouldery scramble up the bilberry slope alongside Rest Gill, and a series of stony rises then leads to the top; this is a rough but interesting route, suitable only in fine weather.

Tongue Pot

Heron Crag

River Esk

1000

900

800

600

700

Yew Crags

Roman Camp

Pillar Pot

stile

500

1000

400

Brotherilkeld

● The usual route proceeds to Three Tarns and then follows the ridge, so taking the fullest advantage of paths. The section between Rest Gill and Three Tarns is rough, but most ingeniously and delightfully cairned.

● The easiest route follows Swinsty Gill up into Adam-a-Cove. This is everywhere grassy — a surprising weakness in the armour of the Crinkles — and it is just possible to come within a few feet of the summit-cairn without handling rock or treading on stones.

300

kiosk

HARDKNOTT PASS 1½

BOOT 2¼

ROAD

looking north-east

ASCENT FROM COCKLEY BECK BRIDGE
2350 feet of ascent : 3 miles

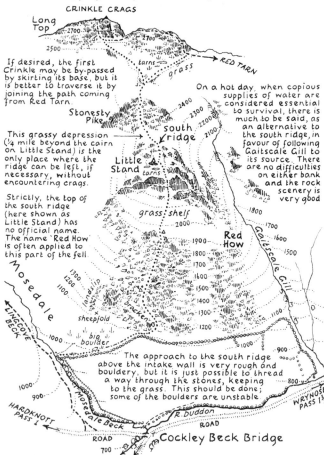

CRINKLE CRAGS

Long Top

2700

2700

2500

tarns

grass

RED TARN

If desired, the first Crinkle may be by-passed by skirting its base, but it is better to traverse it by joining the path coming from Red Tarn.

Stonesty Pike

South Ridge

2400
2300
2200
2100

On a hot day, when copious supplies of water are considered essential to survival, there is much to be said, as an alternative to the south ridge, in favour of following Gaitscale Gill to its source. There are no difficulties on either bank and the rock scenery is very good

This grassy depression (¼ mile beyond the cairn on Little Stand) is the only place where the ridge can be left, if necessary, without encountering crags.

Little Stand

tarns

Strictly, the top of the south ridge (here shown as Little Stand) has no official name. The name 'Red How' is often applied to this part of the fell.

grass shelf

2000

Red How

1800
1900
1800
1700
1600

1800
1700
1600
1500

Moasedale

Lingcove Beck

1300
1200
1100

landslip

bracken

sheepfold

big boulder

1000

1500
1400
1300
1200

1300
1200

1100
1000

900

The approach to the south ridge above the intake wall is very rough and bouldery, but it is just possible to thread a way through the stones, keeping to the grass. This should be done; some of the boulders are unstable.

1000

900

Moasedale Beck

800

WRYNOSE PASS 1½

HARDKNOTT PASS 1

R. Duddon

ROAD

ROAD

700

Cockley Beck Bridge

looking north

DUDDON VALLEY

The scenery of the south ridge is good, with crags and outcrops in abundance, but the approach is fatiguing. This route should not be attempted in bad weather: there is no path to, or on, the ridge, which has escarpments on both flanks.

ASCENT FROM WRYNOSE PASS
1650 feet of ascent : 2¾ miles

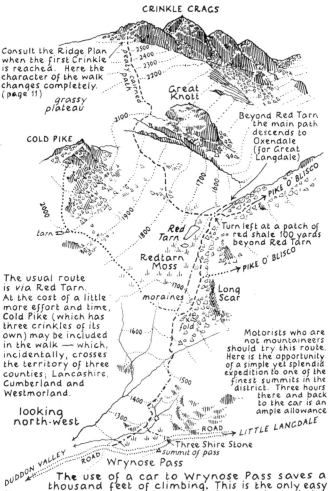

CRINKLE CRAGS

Consult the Ridge Plan when the first Crinkle is reached. Here the character of the walk changes completely. (page 11)

2500
2400
2300
2200

peaty cairned path

grassy plateau

Great Knott

Beyond Red Tarn the main path descends to Oxendale (for Great Langdale)

COLD PIKE

2100

2000

1900

1800

1700

1600

PIKE O' BLISCO

tarn

Red Tarn

Turn left at a patch of red shale 100 yards beyond Red Tarn

Redtarn Moss

PIKE O' BLISCO

The usual route is via Red Tarn. At the cost of a little more effort and time, Cold Pike (which has three crinkles of its own) may be included in the walk — which, incidentally, crosses the territory of three counties; Lancashire, Cumberland and Westmorland.

1700

moraines

Long Scar

fold

1600

Motorists who are not mountaineers should try this route. Here is the opportunity of a simple yet splendid expedition to one of the finest summits in the district. Three hours there and back to the car is an ample allowance.

1500

looking north-west

1400

1300

ROAD

LITTLE LANGDALE

DUDDON VALLEY

ROAD

Wrynose Pass

Three Shire Stone
summit of pass

The use of a car to Wrynose Pass saves a thousand feet of climbing. This is the only easy line of approach to Crinkle Crags, the gradients being gentle and the walking pleasant throughout.

RIDGE PLAN
for use when traversing the ridge from SOUTH to NORTH

● Read upwards from the bottom

All heights ending in 0 are approximate and unofficial

N

ONE MILE

BOWFELL

GREAT LANGDALE (via THE BAND)

Three Tarns 2320'

ESKDALE

OXENDALE (via HELL GILL)

pools

rocky pool rock slabs

2400'

2540' prominent rock tower

grassy depression 2500'

stony depression 2550'

gully (no way down)

2631'

Shelter Crags

spring 2670' tarns

stepping stones 2650'
2680'

to ESKDALE path (keep on north bank of Rest Gill)

depression 2600'

tarn

OXENDALE (direct route)

● fifth Crinkle — cairn 20 yards east of path; boulders on top.

depression 2650'

Fifth Crinkle, 2680' (Gunson Knott)

● fourth Crinkle — cairn 10 yards east of path on edge of crags; excellent view of Langdale.

fourth Crinkle, 2730'

● third Crinkle — cairn 50 yards east of path on easy ground.

third Crinkle, 2740'

Mickle Door (wide scree gully)

● second Crinkle — see summit notes for details

second (and highest) Crinkle, 2816'

grassy rake
Bad Step

OXENDALE via CRINKLE GILL

grassy depression 2630'

scree slide

scree slide

Great Cove

ADAM-A-COVE

● first Crinkle — several cairns; this is the longest Crinkle (350 yards); views down two gullies on the right

first Crinkle, 2733'

gullies

view across Great Cove of second and third Crinkles with Mickle Door between

2550'

SOUTH RIDGE

RED TARN

This ridge is a fell-walkers' delight. A constantly changing scene, beautiful and dramatic views, fine situations and an interesting course throughout make this a walk to remember.

Looking NORTH along the ridge ....

The second (and highest)
Crinkle, Mickle Door,
and the third Crinkle,
seen across Great Cove

The fourth and fifth
Crinkles (Shelter Crags
and Bowfell behind), seen
from the third Crinkle

RIDGE PLAN
for use when traversing the ridge from NORTH to SOUTH

• **Read upwards from the bottom**

This is, of course, the same plan as that already given for the south-to-north traverse but reversed for easier reference. Reading upwards, left and right on the plan will agree with left and right as they appear to the walker

All heights ending in 0 are approximate and unofficial.

RED SCREE

SOUTH RIDGE

RED TARN 2550'

viewpoint "X" (fourth and third Crinkles, with Mickle Door between)

gullies

Great Cove

← **fifth Crinkle, 2733'** — the longest Crinkle; several cairns along its top

grassy depression 2630' → ADAM-A-COVE

Bad Step ┈ grassy rake

OXENDALE via CRINKLE GILL →

fourth (and highest) Crinkle
Mickle Door (wide scree gully)

• **fourth Crinkle** — see summit notes for detail

2816'

third Crinkle, 2740' →

• **third Crinkle** — cairn 50 ya east of path on easy ground

second Crinkle, 2730' →

• **second Crinkle** — cairn o edge of crags 10 yards east of path excellent view of Langdale

first Crinkle, 2680' (Gunson Knott)

2650' tarn

• **first Crinkle** — cairn 20 ya east of path; boulders (shelter) on top

OXENDALE (direct route) ← 2600'

→ easy route to ESKDALE path (keep on north bank of Rest Gill)

first four Crinkles all came into sight

tarns 2670' stepping stones 2650'

2650'

Shelter Crags 2631' ×spring

Note that the arrow is upside-down, too

gully 2550' **stony depression**

2500' grassy depression

prominent rock tower 2540'

2400'

rock slabs rocky pool pools

ESKDALE →

OXENDALE (via HELL GILL) ←

○ Three ○ Tarns 2320'

HALF A MILE

N

GREAT LANGDALE (via THE BAND)

BOWFELL

Some writer have greatl exaggerate the danger of the ridge Nowhere is anything bu a pleasantl rough walk except fo the Bad Ste which ca be avoided (Bowfell an Scafell Pik are roughe

---

Introducing Lakeland's best ridge-mile!

Looking SOUTH along the ridge ....

Four Crinkles come
suddenly into view from
the path as it rounds a
corner of Shelter Crags

The fifth Crinkle
as seen from the main
Crinkle on the descent
to the Bad Step

THE SUMMIT

← BOWFELL

There are five Crinkles (not counting Shelter Crags) an
therefore five summits, each with its own summit-cairn
The highest is, however, so obviously the highest that th
true top of the fell is not in doubt in clear visibility, an
this is the Crinkle (the fourth from the north and secon
from the south) with which these notes are concerned. I
is not the stoniest of the five, nor the greatest in girth
but, unlike the others, it extends a considerable distance
as a lateral ridge (Long Top) descending westwards.   O
the actual summit are two principal cairns separated b
40 yards of easy ground; that to the north, standing on
rock platform, is slightly the more elevated. The easter
face descends in precipices from the easy grass terrace
above it; there are crags running down steeply from th
south cairn also, but in other directions the top terrai
is not difficult although everywhere rough.

1 : grassy rake (easy way)
2 : direct route (steep scree)
3 : the Bad Step (see next page)
4 : detour to avoid the Bad Step

The highest Crinkle, from the south

continued

THE SUMMIT

continued

DESCENTS

GREAT LANGDALE : The orthodox routes are (1) *via* Red Tarn and Brown How, and (2) *via* Three Tarns and the Band, both excellent walks, and in normal circumstances no other ways should be considered. If time is very short, however, or if it is necessary to escape quickly from stormy conditions on the ridge, quick and sheltered routes are provided by (3) the scree gully of Mickle Door or (4) the Gunson Knott gully, which is easier : both are very rough initially but lead to open slopes above Oxendale.

ESKDALE : Much the easiest way, and much the quickest, is to descend from Adam-a-Cove (no path), keeping *left* of Swinsty Gill where it enters a ravine. Long Top is a temptation to be resisted, for it leads only to trouble.

COCKLEY BECK BRIDGE : The south ridge is interesting (no path and not safe in mist), but tired limbs had better take advantage of the easy way down from Adam-a-Cove, inclining *left* below Rey Crag into Mosedale.

WRYNOSE PASS : Reverse the route of ascent. Cold Pike may be traversed with little extra cost in energy.

In mist, take good care to keep to the ridge-path, which, in many places, is no more than nail-scratches on rocks and boulders but is generally simple to follow. Go nowhere unless there is evidence that many others have passed that way before. (The exception to this golden rule is Adam-a-Cove, which is perfectly safe *if it is remembered to keep to the left bank of the stream*).

The Bad Step

Caution is needed on the descent southwards from the summit. A walker crossing the top from the north will naturally gravitate to the south cairn and start his descent here. A steep path goes down rock ledges to a slope of loose scree, which spills over the top of a chockstone (two, really) bridging and blocking a little gully. Anyone descending at speed here is asking for a nasty fall. The impasse is usually avoided and the gully regained below the chockstone by an awkward descent of the rock wall to the left, which deserves the name 'The Bad Step', for it is 10 feet high and as near vertical as makes no difference. This is the sort of place that everybody would get down in a flash if a £5 note was waiting to be picked up on the scree below, but, without such an inducement, there is much wavering on the brink. Chicken-hearted walkers, muttering something about discretion being the better part of valour, will sneak away and circumvent the difficulty by following the author's footsteps round the left flank of the buttress forming the retaining wall of the gully, where grassy ledges enable the foot of the gully to be reached without trouble; here they may sit and watch, with ill-concealed grins, the discomfiture of other tourists who may come along.

The Bad Step is the most difficult obstacle met on any of the regular walkers' paths in Lakeland.

*The Bad Step
from below*

continued

THE SUMMIT

continued

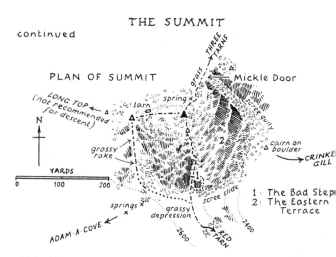

PLAN OF SUMMIT

LONG TOP ← (not recommended for descent)

Mickle Door

1: The Bad Step
2: The Eastern Terrace

YARDS
0   100   200

CRINKLE GILL

ADAM·A·COVE

RED TARN

Note that the steep direct descent from the south cairn may be by-passed altogether (it was formerly customary to do so) by proceeding west from the main cairn for 140 yards to another on grass in a slight depression, whence a grassy rake on the left goes down, skirting completely the rocks of the Crinkle to join the direct route at its base

The welcome spring on the summit (usually reliable after recent rain) is remarkable for its proximity to the top cairn (30 yards north-east, in the bend of the path); it is only 20 feet lower than the cairn, and has a very limited gathering-ground. Find it by listening for it — it emerges as a tiny waterfall from beneath a boulder. This is not the highest spring in the district but it is the nearest to a high summit.

The Eastern Terrace

A conspicuous grass terrace slants at an angle of 30° across the eastern cliffs of the main Crinkle, rising from the screes of the Mickle Door gully to the direct ridge-route just above the Bad Step. It is not seen from the ridge but appears in views of the east face clearly, being the middle of three such terraces and most prominent. It is of little use to walkers, except those who (in defiance of advice already given) are approaching the summit from Crinkle Gill: for them it offers a way of escape from the final screes. The terrace (identified by a little wall at the side of the gully) is wide and without difficulties but is no place for loitering, being subject to bombardments of stones by bloody fools, if any, on the summit above. It is well to remember, too, that the terrace is bounded by a precipice. At the upper end the terrace becomes more broken near the Bad Step and is not quite easy to locate when approached from this direction.

1: the Bad Step
2: the Eastern Terrace
3: Mickle Door
4: scree slide

cairn on boulder

The Eastern Face

RIDGE ROUTES

To BOWFELL, 2960': 1½ miles: Generally N, then WNW
Five depressions; final one (Three Tarns) at 2320': 850 feet of ascent
Positively one of the finest ridge-walks in Lakeland.

The rough stony ground makes progress slow, but this walk is,
in any case, deserving of a leisurely appreciation; it is much too
good to be done in a hurry. Every turn of the fairly distinct track
is interesting, and in places even exciting, although no difficulty
is met except for an occasional awkward stride on rock.   In
mist, the walker will probably have to descend to Three Tarns
anyway, but should give Bowfell a miss, especially if the route
is unfamiliar.

Bowfell, as seen on the
descent from Shelter Crags

ONE MILE

N

CRINKLE CRAGS

BOWFELL
Flat
Crags
Bowfell
Links
Three
Tarns
GREAT
LANGDALE
ESKDALE
Shelter
Crags
CRINKLE CRAGS

To COLD PIKE, 2259':
1½ miles: SE
Depressions at 2625' and 2100'
300 feet of ascent
Interesting and dull in patches

RED TARN

COLD
PIKE

Consult the summit notes before starting.
After the splendid traverse of the final
Crinkle, the nature of the surroundings
changes completely and a large grassy
plateau stretches ahead: this may be
crossed in a beeline, but it is preferable, especially after rain, to
keep to the Red Tarn path until a gentle slope, becoming craggy,
leads easily to the attractive triple summit of Cold Pike.

THE VIEW

The view is not quite as comprehensive as might be expected, the western and north-western fells (with the exception of Eel Crag) being out of sight behind the bulky Scafell group and Bowfell, but is excellent nevertheless. Of special distinction is the supremely beautiful view of the valleys of the Duddon and the Esk winding down to the sea: from no other summit are they so well seen. There is a more dramatic but less attractive picture of Great Langdale, best seen from the edge of the eastern cliffs.

Intruding in the fine array of mountains and lakes and valleys and sea is a comparatively new feature—the cooling towers of the Calder Hall atomic power station, neatly framed in the dip of the skyline between Whin Rigg and Illgill Head, the two heights above Wastwater Screes. The summit of Crinkle Crags is ageless, the cooling towers are symbols of one particular age. Here, on this rugged mountain-top, is an everlasting permanence, something simple, and we can understand; but *there*, on the horizon, is something that is temporary, and complicated beyond our comprehension. Those modern structures, out of place in a landscape that is constant and unchanging, will vanish from the scene with the passing years. The mountains, nature's symbols of power and strength, will remain.

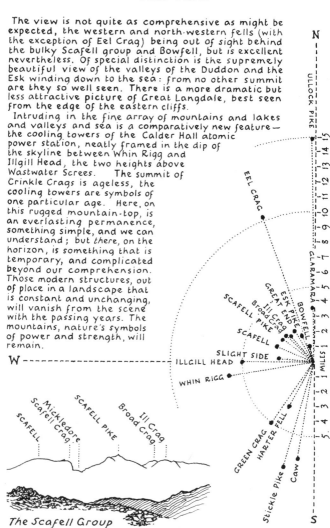

The Scafell Group

THE VIEW

Principal Fells

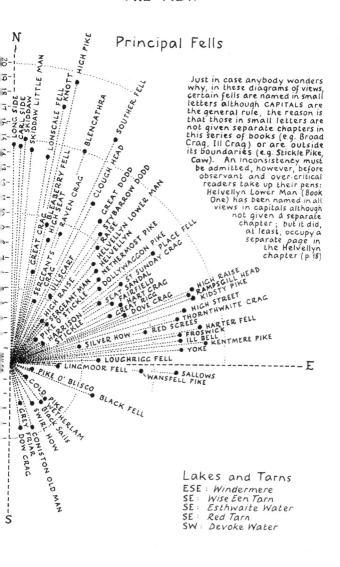

Just in case anybody wonders why, in these diagrams of views, certain fells are named in small letters although CAPITALS are the general rule, the reason is that those in small letters are not given separate chapters in this series of books (e.g. Broad Crag, Ill Crag) or are outside its boundaries (e.g. Stickle Pike, Caw). An inconsistency must be admitted, however, before observant and over-critical readers take up their pens: Helvellyn Lower Man (Book One) has been named in all views in capitals although not given a separate chapter; but it did, at least, occupy a separate page in the Helvellyn chapter (p.18)

Lakes and Tarns

ESE : *Windermere*
SE : *Wise Een Tarn*
SE : *Esthwaite Water*
SE : *Red Tarn*
SW : *Devoke Water*

Great Gable

2949

from Wastwater

NATURAL FEATURES

Great Gable is a favourite of all fellwalkers, and first favourite with many. Right from the start of one's apprenticeship in the hills, the name appeals magically. It is a good name for a mountain, strong, challenging, compelling, starkly descriptive, suggesting the pyramid associated with the shape of mountains since early childhood.   People are attracted to it because of the name.   There is satisfaction in having achieved the ascent and satisfaction in announcing the fact to others.   The name has status, and confers status... Yes, the name is good, simple yet subtly clever. If Great Gable were known only as Wasdale Fell fewer persons would climb it.

continued

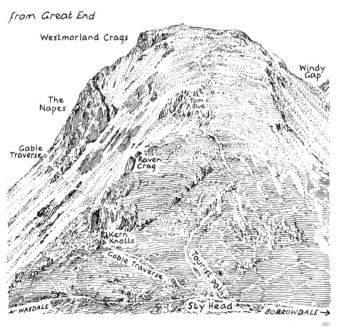

from Great End

Westmorland Crags

Windy Gap

The Napes

Tom Blue

Gable Traverse

Raven Crag

Kern Knotts

Gable Traverse

Tourist Path

←WASDALE

Sty Head

BORROWDALE→

NATURAL FEATURES

continued

In appearance, too, Great Gable has the same appealing attributes. The name fits well. This mountain is strong yet not sturdy, masculine yet graceful. It is the undisputed overlord of the group of hills to which it belongs, and its superior height is emphasised tremendously by the deep gulf separating it from the Scafells and allowing an impressive view that reveals the whole of its half-mile altitude as an unremitting and unbroken pyramid: this is the aspect of the fell that earned the name. From east and west the slender tapering of the summit as seen from the south is not in evidence, the top appearing as a massive square-cut dome. From the north, where the build-up of height is more gradual, the skyline is a symmetrical arc.

continued

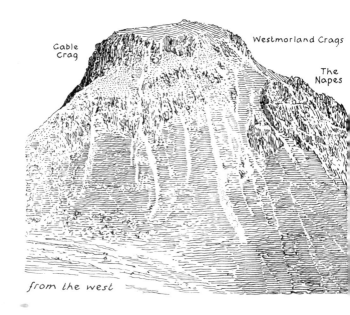

Cable Crag

Westmorland Crags

The Napes

from the west

NATURAL FEATURES

continued

Great Gable is a desert of stones. Vegetation is scanty, feeding few sheep. Petrified rivers of scree scar the southern slopes, from which stand out the bony ribs of the Napes ridges; the whole fell on this side is a sterile wilderness, dry and arid and dusty. The north face is a shadowed precipice, Gable Crag. Slopes to east and west are rough and stony. In some lights, especially in the afterglow of sunset, Great Gable is truly a beautiful mountain, but it is never a pretty one.

The view from the top is far-reaching, but not quite in balance because of the nearness of the Scafells, which, however, are seen magnificently. The aerial aspect of Wasdale is often described as the finest view in the district, a claim that more witnesses will accept than will dispute.

continued

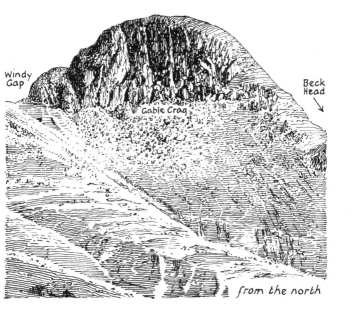

Windy Gap

Gable Crag

Beck Head

from the north

NATURAL FEATURES
continued

The failing of Great Gable is that it holds few mysteries, all its wares being openly displayed. The explorer, the man who likes to look around corners and discover secrets and intimacies, may be disappointed, not on a first visit, which cannot fail to be interesting, but on subsequent occasions. There are no cavernous recesses, no hidden tarns, no combes, no hanging valleys, no waterfalls, no streams other than those forming the boundaries.

Yet walkers tread its familiar tracks again and again, almost as a ritual, and climbers queue to scale its familiar rocks. The truth is, Great Gable casts a spell. It starts as an honourable adversary and becomes a friend. The choice of its summit as a war memorial is testimony to the affection and respect felt for this grand old mountain.

• Gatesgarth
Honister
Pass ╳   Seatoller

)(Scarth
Gap Pass   ▲ GREY KNOTTS
▲ BRANDRETH
Black Sail   ● Seathwaite
// Pass   ▲ BASE BROWN
                   ▲ GREEN GABLE
KIRK ▲   ▲ GREAT GABLE
FELL
                   // Sty Head Pass
● Wasdale Head

MILES

0   1   2   3

Dry Tarn

This is a tarn that Nature fashioned and forgot. It is invariably bone-dry although mossy stones indicate the former presence of water. Dry Tarn is almost unknown, yet is within sight of the main path up Great Gable from Sty Head, being situated at 2100 feet on a grass shelf: it is more likely to be seen when descending.
This is Great Gable's only tarn.

MAP

Crags and other features are shown in greater detail, and named, on the larger-scale maps and diagrams appearing elsewhere in this chapter.

A curious thing about Great Gable is that, although of commanding height and so far overtopping the supporting fells as to seem to rise in isolation, it is really a huge cone resting on a high land-mass. Great Gable overlooks many valleys and waters three, yet it has no roots in any except Wasdale; even here its foothold is ineffectual, being a mile beyond the true head of the valley in a side-opening. On all other flanks, it is a mountain hoisted on the shoulders of supporters that have direct valley links and take over the function of principal buttresses.

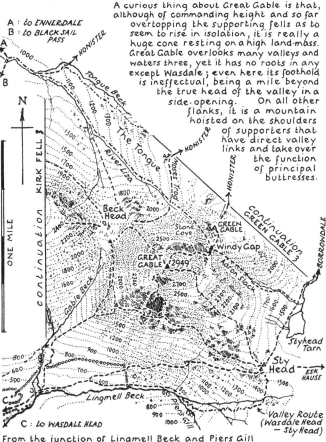

A : to ENNERDALE
B : to BLACK SAIL PASS

C : to WASDALE HEAD

From the junction of Lingmell Beck and Piers Gill the summit is two-thirds of a mile north in lateral distance and the difference in altitude is 2,200 feet, a gradient of 1 in 1⅗. This is the longest slope in the district of such continuous and concentrated steepness.

Moses' Trod

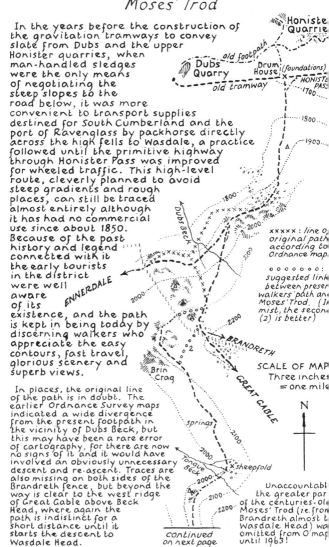

In the years before the construction of the gravitation tramways to convey slate from Dubs and the upper Honister quarries, when man-handled sledges were the only means of negotiating the steep slopes to the road below, it was more convenient to transport supplies destined for South Cumberland and the port of Ravenglass by packhorse directly across the high fells to Wasdale, a practice followed until the primitive highway through Honister Pass was improved for wheeled traffic. This high-level route, cleverly planned to avoid steep gradients and rough places, can still be traced almost entirely although it has had no commercial use since about 1850. Because of the past history and legend connected with it the early tourists in the district were well aware of its existence, and the path is kept in being today by discerning walkers who appreciate the easy contours, fast travel, glorious scenery and superb views.

In places, the original line of the path is in doubt. The earlier Ordnance Survey maps indicated a wide divergence from the present footpath in the vicinity of Dubs Beck, but this may have been a rare error of cartography, for there are now no signs of it and it would have involved an obviously unnecessary descent and re-ascent. Traces are also missing on both sides of the Brandreth fence, but beyond the way is clear to the west ridge of Great Gable above Beck Head, where again the path is indistinct for a short distance until it starts the descent to Wasdale Head.

Honister Quarries

old footpath

Dubs Quarry

Drum House (foundations)

old tramway

HONISTER PASS 1700

1800

1900

Dubs Beck

1800

2000

2100

xxxxx : line of original path according to Ordnance map.

ENNERDALE

2000

o o o o o o o o : suggested link between present walkers' path and Moses' Trod. (In mist, the second (2) is better)

2200

BRANDRETH

SCALE OF MAP
Three inches = one mile

GREAT GABLE

N

Brin Crag

springs

2100

2000

Tongue Beck

2000

sheepfold

2100

2200

Unaccountably the greater part of the centuries-old Moses' Trod (i.e. from Brandreth almost to Wasdale Head) was omitted from O. maps until 1963!

continued on next page

Moses' Trod

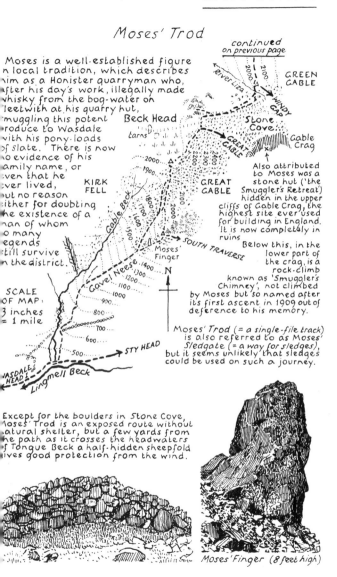

continued on previous page

Moses is a well-established figure in local tradition, which describes him as a Honister quarryman who, after his day's work, illegally made whisky from the bog-water on Fleetwith at his quarry hut, smuggling this potent produce to Wasdale with his pony-loads of slate. There is now no evidence of his family name, or even that he ever lived, but no reason either for doubting the existence of a man of whom so many legends still survive in the district.

Also attributed to Moses was a stone hut ('the Smuggler's Retreat') hidden in the upper cliffs of Gable Crag, the highest site ever used for building in England. It is now completely in ruins

Below this, in the lower part of the crag, is a rock-climb known as 'Smuggler's Chimney', not climbed by Moses but so named after its first ascent in 1909 out of deference to his memory.

Moses' Trod (= a single-file track) is also referred to as Moses' Sledgate (= a way for sledges), but it seems unlikely that sledges could be used on such a journey.

SCALE OF MAP:
3 inches = 1 mile

Except for the boulders in Stone Cove, Moses' Trod is an exposed route without natural shelter, but a few yards from the path as it crosses the headwaters of Tongue Beck a half-hidden sheepfold gives good protection from the wind.

Moses' Finger (8 feet high)

The Gable Girdle
(linking the South Traverse and the North Traverse)

Originally a track for a privileged few (i.e. the early rock-climbers) the South Traverse, rising across the flank of Great Gable from Sty Head, has now become a much-fancied way for lesser fry (i.e. modern hikers). The North Traverse passes immediately below the base of Gable Crag, and although still largely the province of climbers is equally accessible to walkers. The two traverses can be linked on the west by tracks over the scree above Beck Head; to the east the North Traverse is continued by the regular path down Aaron Slack to Sty Head. It is thus possible for walkers to make a full circuit of the mountain through interesting territory with fairly distinct tracks underfoot the whole way.

This is the finest mountain walk in the district that does not aim to reach a summit.

It is not level going: the route lies between 1500' and 2500', with many ups and downs. There are rough places to negotiate and nasty scree to cross and climb, but no dangers or difficulties. It is a doddle compared with, say, Jack's Rake or even Lord's Rake. Here one never has the feeling that the end is nigh.

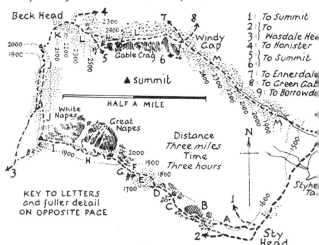

Beck Head

2300
2400

Windy Gap

2000
1900

5 Gable Crag 6

▲ Summit

HALF A MILE

White Napes

Great Napes

Distance
Three miles
Time
Three hours

1900   2000

H   F   1900
G   1800

1700

KEY TO LETTERS
and fuller detail
ON OPPOSITE PAGE

N

1600

1500

Styhead
Tarn

Sty Head

1: To Summit
2: } To
3: } Wasdale Head
4: To Honister
5: } To Summit
6: }
7: To Ennerdale
8: To Green Gable
9: To Borrowdale

Boots, not shoes, should be worn, and they must have soles with a firm grip, or there will be trouble on the boulders. There are few sections where the splendid views may be admired while walking: always stop to look around. The route is almost sheep-free, and dogs may be taken. So may small children, who are natural scramblers, and well-behaved women, but nagging wives should be left to paddle their feet in Styhead Tarn. The journey demands and deserves concentration.

The Gable Girdle

The South Traverse leaves Sty Head near the stretcher box, by a
distinct stony path slanting left of the direct route up the mountain.
There has been a big change here in the last twenty years. At one
time, when the Traverse was the exclusive preserve of climbers, the
commencement at Sty Head was deliberately kept obscure, so that
walkers bound for the summit direct would not be beguiled along a
false trail. But now the start is clearer than the start of the direct
route, and many walkers enter upon it in the belief that it will lead
them to the top of the mountain. It won't, not without a lot of effort.

KEY TO THE MAP ON THE OPPOSITE PAGE:

Sty Head to Kern Knotts:

A : Undulating path over grassy alps
    to bouldery depression and stony
    rise to the base of the crag.

B : Huge boulders to be negotiated
    along the base of the crag. [A
    simpler variation passes below
    these boulders (good shelter here)
    and climbs roughly up the far side]

High
Kern
Knotts

Kern Knotts to Great Hell Gate:

C : Horizontal track over boulders
    leads to easier ground. A small
    hollow is skirted (boulders again)
    after which there is a short rise
    to a rocky corner.

D : A cave on the right provides a
    trickle of water (the last until
    Aaron Slack). A short scramble
    up rocky steps follows.

E : An easy rising path on scree.

F : The head of two gullies is
    crossed on rocky slabs.

G : Easy rising path to Great
    Hell Gate (a scree shoot).
    Tophet Wall in view ahead.

Great Hell Gate to Little Hell Gate:

H : A section of some confusion,
    resolved by referring to the
    next page following.

Little Hell Gate to Beck Head:

I : The scree-shoot of Little Hell Gate
    is crossed and a track picked up
    opposite: this trends downwards
    to a cairn at the angle of the south
    and west faces. Here endeth the
    South Traverse. [A scree-path goes
    down to Wasdale Head at this point]

J : Around the grassy corner a thin
    trod contours the west slope and
    joins a clear track rising to Beck
    Head (cairn on a boulder).

The water-hole (D)

Beck Head to Windy Gap:

K : Skirt the marshy ground ahead
    to a slanting scree-path rising to
    the angle of the north and west
    faces. [Moses' Trod goes off to the
    left here by a small pool]

L : The steep loose scree of the north-west ridge is climbed for 100 yds.
    Watch closely for two cairns forming a 'gateway' (illustrated on page 27).
    Here commenceth the North Traverse. A track runs along the base of
    Gable Crag, descending to round the lowest buttress and then rising
    across scree to Windy Gap.

Windy Gap to Sty Head:

M : A popular tourist path descends Aaron Slack to Styhead Tarn, where,
    if women are found paddling their feet, a greeting may be unwise.

The Great Napes

Rock climbers have played a much
greater part than walkers in the
selection of identifying names
for natural features. All the
names of the Great Napes
are attributable to those
who carried out the first
exploration of the crags.
Fortunately
their choice
was always
appropriate,
descriptive,
and often
inspired.

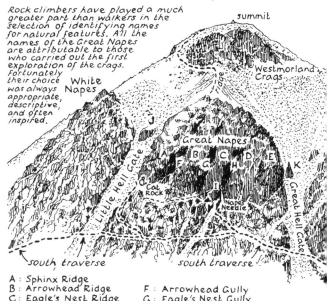

A : Sphinx Ridge
B : Arrowhead Ridge
C : Eagle's Nest Ridge
D : Needle Ridge
E : Tophet Bastion

F : Arrowhead Gully
G : Eagle's Nest Gully
H : Needle Gully   J : rock island
I : Dress Circle   K : Hell Gate Pillar

The Great Napes is a rocky excrescence high on the southern
flank of Great Gable. Unlike most crags, which buttress and
merge into the general slope of a mountain, the Great Napes
rises like a castle above its surroundings so that there is not
only a front wall of rock but side walls and a back wall too. This
elevated mass is cut into by gullies to form four ridges, three of
slender proportions and the fourth, and most easterly, broad-
based and of substantial girth. The steepest rock occurs in the
eastern part, the ground generally becoming more broken to the
west. The front of the ridges, facing Wasdale, springs up almost
vertically, but the gradient eases after the initial steepness to
give grassy ledges in the higher reaches; the gullies, too, lose
their sharp definition towards the top. Gradually the upper
extremities of the Napes rise to a common apex, and here, at
this point only, the Napes is undefended and a simple, grassy,
and quite delightful ridge links with the main body of the fell.
Here a climber may walk off the Napes and a walker may enter,
with care, upon the easier upper heights. From the link ridge
wide channels of scree pour down both sides of the Napes, thus
defining the area clearly.
Across the westerly scree-channel the rocky tower of the White
Napes emphasises the angle of the south and west faces of the
mountain but has no notable crags and little of interest.

The Great Napes

continued

The South Traverse reaches its highest elevation in the section of about 250 yards between the two Hell Gates and beneath the Great Napes, but it does not venture to the base of the wall of crags, preferring an easier passage 50-80 yards lower down the slope, where it maintains a horizontal course on the 2000' contour. The intervening ground is steep and rocky, especially in the vicinity of the Needle, and its exploration calls for care. The Needle is in full view from the Traverse but does not seem its usual self (as usually seen in illustrations) and on a dull day is not easily distinguished from its background of rock. To visit it, take the rising branch-path from the Traverse into Needle Gully, and go up this to the base of the pinnacle; a crumbling track opposite climbs up to a ledge known as the Dress Circle, the traditional balcony for watching the ascent of the Needle. From this ledge a higher traverse can be made along the base of the crags, going below the Cat Rock into Little Hell Gate, but there is a tricky section initially and this is no walk for dogs, small children, well-behaved women and the like.

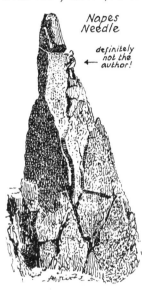

Napes
Needle

← definitely
  not the
  author!

Midway between the two Hell Gates Needle Gully and a branch gully, full of scree, cut across the South Traverse, which otherwise hereabouts is mainly a matter of rounding little buttresses. Another bifurcation leads off to Little Hell Gate at a higher level, near the Cat Rock. If proceeding west (i.e. from Sty Head) the two rising branch-paths may be followed by mistake without realising that the Traverse has been left, they being the more distinct, a circumstance that does not arise when proceeding east.

ROUTES TO THE SUMMIT FROM THE SOUTH TRAVERSE

It is no uncommon thing for walkers to venture upon the South Traverse, from Sty Head, in the fond hope that it will lead them in due course to the summit of Great Gable. This hope is dashed when the Napes is reached, for here the path becomes uncertain and the rocks are an impassable obstacle. The clue to further ascent is provided when it is remembered that 'gate' is a local word for 'way' and that the Napes is bounded by the two Hell Gates. Either of these will conduct the walker safely upwards, but both are chutes for loose stones and steep and arduous to climb. In Little Hell Gate it is possible, with care, to scramble off the scree onto Sphinx Ridge at several points). The two routes converge at the little ridge below Westmorland Crags, which are rounded on the left by a good track that winds up to the summit plateau.

The Cat Rock

The
Sphinx
Rock

This is the same pinnacle, shown here from the two angles that have given the two names

The Great Napes

left:
Tophet Bastion
as seen from the
South Traverse
on the approach
from Sty Head.
   The scree of
Great Hell Gate
runs down to the
bottom left.

below:
   looking steeply
down on Tophet
Bastion and the
upper wall of the
Napes, with the
scree of Great Hell
Gate running down
to the left, from
Westmorland Cairn

The Great Napes

Eagle's Nest Gully

Eagle's Nest Ridge
(lower part known as Abbey Buttress)

looking upwards from just above the South Traverse

Needle Gully

Needle Ridge

Napes Needle

rock island

Westmorland Crags

looking up Little Hell Gate

Tophet Bastion

Hell Gate Pillar

looking up Great Hell Gate

ASCENT FROM SEATHWAITE
2700 feet of ascent
2¾ miles

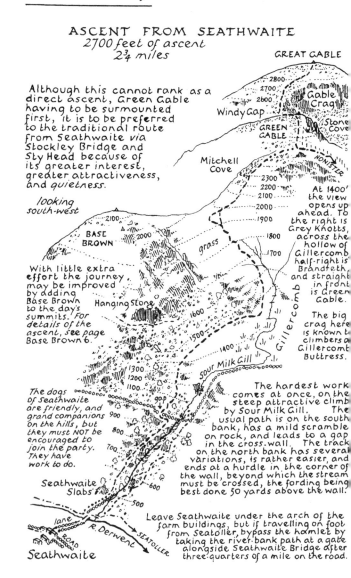

GREAT GABLE

Although this cannot rank as a direct ascent, Green Gable having to be surmounted first, it is to be preferred to the traditional route from Seathwaite via Stockley Bridge and Sty Head because of its greater interest, greater attractiveness, and *quietness*.

looking south-west

2800
2700
2600
Gable Crag

Windy Gap

GREEN GABLE

Stone Cove

Mitchell Cove

HONISTER

2300
2200
2100
2000
1900
1800
1700

At 1400' the view opens up ahead. To the right is Grey Knotts, across the hollow of Gillercomb half-right is Brandreth and straight in front is Green Gable.

BASE BROWN

2100
2000

grass

With little extra effort the journey may be improved by adding Base Brown to the day's summits. For details of the ascent, see page Base Brown 6.

Hanging Stone

1600

1500

1400

Gillercomb

The big crag here is known to climbers as Gillercomb Buttress.

The dogs of Seathwaite are friendly, and grand companions on the hills, but they must NOT be encouraged to join the party. They have work to do.

1300
1200
1100

gap

900

800

700

Sour Milk Gill

The hardest work comes at once, on the steep attractive climb by Sour Milk Gill. The usual path is on the south bank, has a mild scramble on rock, and leads to a gap in the cross-wall. The track on the north bank has several variations, is rather easier, and ends at a hurdle in the corner of the wall, beyond which the stream must be crossed, the fording being best done 50 yards above the wall.

Seathwaite Slabs

600

500

lane

ROAD

R. Derwent

SEATOLLER

Seathwaite

Leave Seathwaite under the arch of the farm buildings, but if travelling on foot from Seatoller, bypass the hamlet by taking the river-bank path at a gate alongside Seathwaite Bridge after three-quarters of a mile on the road.

ASCENT FROM STY HEAD
1350 feet of ascent : 1 mile
(from Wasdale Head: 2750 feet : ¾ miles
from Seathwaite: 2600 feet : 3¼ miles)

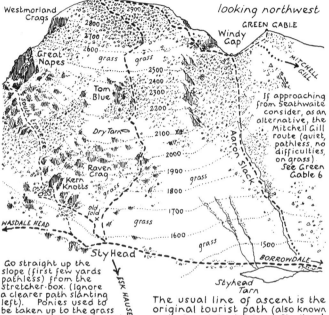

looking northwest

GREAT GABLE

Westmorland Crags

2900
2800
2700
2600
Great Napes

grass   grass

GREEN GABLE

Windy Gap

MITCHELL GILL

Tom Blue

2500
2400
2300
2200

Dry Tarn

2100

2000

Raven Crag

1900

grass

Kern Knotts

1800

grass

1700

old fold ×

grass

1600

Aaron Slack

If approaching from Seathwaite consider, as an alternative, the Mitchell Gill route (quiet, pathless, no difficulties, on grass) See Green Gable 6

WASDALE HEAD

grass

Sty Head

ESK HAUSE

grass

1500

BORROWDALE

Styhead Tarn

Go straight up the slope (first few yards pathless) from the stretcher-box. (Ignore a clearer path slanting left). Ponies used to be taken up to the grass shelf at 2500', but the path was then in a better state!

The usual line of ascent is the original tourist path (also known as the Breast Route) from Sty Head. It is abundantly cairned, safe in mist, but very bad underfoot (loose scree) on the steep rise by Tom Blue, where clumsy walkers have utterly ruined the path. The Aaron Slack route gives a rather firmer footing.

There are good walkers and bad walkers, and the difference between them has nothing to do with performances in mileage or speed. The difference lies in the way they put their feet down.

A good walker is a *tidy* walker. He moves quietly, places his feet where his eyes tell him to, on beaten tracks treads firmly, avoids loose stones on steep ground, disturbs nothing. He is, by habit, an improver of paths.

A bad walker is a *clumsy* walker. He moves noisily, disturbs the surface and even the foundations of paths by kicking up loose stones, tramples the verges until they disintegrate into debris. He is, by habit, a maker of bad tracks and a spoiler of good ones.

A good walker's special joy is zigzags, which he follows faithfully. A bad walker's special joy is in shortcutting and destroying zigzags.

All fellwalking accidents are the result of clumsiness.

ASCENT FROM HONISTER PASS
1950 feet of ascent : 3 miles

GREAT GABLE

Windy Gap
GREEN GABLE

Gable Crag

2500
2400

looking
south

2500

2400

Stone Cove

2000

Beck Head

2300

River Liza

2200

The Tongue

2100

Tongue Beck

Gillercomb
Head

Moses Trod

BRANDRETH

2200

2200

grass

2100

2000

ENNERDALE

2200

GREY KNOTTS

2100

1900

grass

1800

The usual route follows
the path over Green
Gable, descends to
Windy Gap and climbs
left of Gable Crag: a
well-blazed trail with
a large population on
any fine day.

Human beings can
be avoided and the
ascent made more
direct (omitting
Green Gable) by
switching over to
Moses' Trod at the
Brandreth west fence
(to join the Trod, aim
across grass south for
200 yards). Follow the
Trod into Stone Cove
where either (a) turn
left up to Windy Gap,
there rejoining the main path,
or (b) continue along the Trod
to the bluff above Beck Head
and there turn up scree to
the summit. If returning
to Honister, use (b), and
come back by the path
over Green Gable.

An initially more strenuous
alternative follows the line
of fenceposts behind the
quarry buildings, passing
over the summits of Grey
Knotts and Brandreth.
There is no path (although
the 1963 1" Ordnance Survey
map shows one) until the usual
route is joined at Gillercomb Head
but the line of posts is an impeccable
guide in any sort of weather; at a
junction of fences on Grey Knotts
keep to the right.

1700

DUBS QUARRY

foundations of
Drum House

1600

sleepers
old tramway

For additional notes relating to
this walk and its surroundings
consult Brandreth 4
Fleetwith Pike 5
Great Gable 7
Green Gable 4
Grey Knotts 7

rock
cutting

1300

quarry
buildings

Youth Hostel

1200

signpost

quarry road

PRIVATE

BUTTERMERE

ROAD

SEATOLLER
1½

Honister Pass
(or Hause)

This is an excellent
route for motorists
who may abandon
their cars on the Pass,
with a height of 1190 feet
already achieved, and
experience the wind on
the heath, brother, for
the next five hours with
no thought of gears and
brakes and clutches and
things, and feel all the
better for exercising his
limbs as nature intended

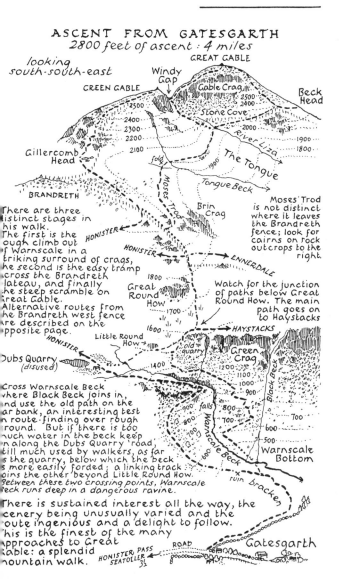

ASCENT FROM GATESGARTH
2800 feet of ascent : 4 miles

looking
south-south-east

GREAT GABLE

GREEN GABLE Windy Gap Gable Crag Beck Head

2500 2400 Stone Cove 2500 2400

Gillercomb Head 2400 2300 2200 2100 fold 2000 River Liza 1900 1800

BRANDRETH 900 The Tongue

Moses Trod Tongue Beck

Brin Crag

Moses' Trod is not distinct where it leaves the Brandreth fence; look for cairns on rock outcrops to the right.

There are three distinct stages in his walk. The first is the rough climb out of Warnscale in a striking surround of crags, the second is the easy tramp across the Brandreth plateau, and finally the steep scramble on Great Gable. Alternative routes from the Brandreth west fence are described on the opposite page.

HONISTER HONISTER ENNERDALE

1800 Great Round How 1700

Watch for the junction of paths below Great Round How. The main path goes on to Haystacks.

1600

HONISTER Little Round How HAYSTACKS

old quarry Green Crag

Dubs Quarry (disused) 1400 1200 1100 1000 900

Cross Warnscale Beck where Black Beck joins in, and use the old path on the far bank, an interesting test in route-finding over rough ground. But if there is too much water in the beck keep on along the Dubs Quarry 'road', still much used by walkers, as far as the quarry, below which the beck is more easily forded; a linking track joins the other beyond Little Round How. Between these two crossing points, Warnscale Beck runs deep in a dangerous ravine.

900 falls 900 800 700 600 500

Warnscale Beck Black Beck

Warnscale Bottom

ruin bracken

There is sustained interest all the way, the scenery being unusually varied and the route ingenious and a delight to follow. This is the finest of the many approaches to Great Gable: a splendid mountain walk.

HONISTER PASS SEATOLLER ROAD Gatesgarth

31

ASCENT FROM ENNERDALE
(BLACK SAIL YOUTH HOSTEL)
2000 feet of ascent : 2¼ miles

GREAT GABLE

Gable Crag

GREEN GABLE
Windy Gap

White Napes

2800
2700
2600
2500
2400
2300

North Traverse

Stone Cove

2300
2200

WASDALE HEAD

KIRK FELL

HONISTER ← Moses Trod 2000

Beck Head

1900
1800
1700
1600
1500
1400
1300
1200
1100
1000

River Liza

The Tongue

Tongue Beck

moraines

Sail Beck

WASDALE HEAD

Black Sail Youth Hostel

ENNERDALE

SCARTH GAP

With Great Gable in full view, directly in front all the way, there are no difficulties of route-finding. Another advantage, which will appeal to hikers with tender hooves, is that, unlike most ways up Gable, grass may be kept underfoot to the last third of a mile. Only then, above Beck Head, are the characteristic slopes of shifting scree encountered. From here on, stones are unavoidable (the firmest footing is found at the angle of this northwest ridge) and the slope is relentlessly rough and steep to the edge of the summit plateau. Here, a short detour along the rim of Gable Crag is more rewarding in scenery and views than a direct course for the top cairn.

Estate, parish and local government boundaries in open country are invariably plotted in a series of straight lines — absolutely straight as if drawn on a map with a ruler, not in curves. The men whose job it was to indicate the boundaries on the ground by the erection of wire fences or stone walls were faithful to their instructions and proceed in dead straight lines whatever the natural obstacle encountered. There is a good example of their fidelity at Beck Head, where the wire fence, now in ruins, originally passed through the middle of the two tarns in the depression.

Difficulties of access to the lonely head of Ennerdale for walkers based elsewhere make this ascent almost the exclusive preserve of those privileged by Y.H.A. membership to stay at the hostel.

looking southeast

ASCENT FROM WASDALE HEAD

2700 feet of ascent
2½ miles

*looking
east-north-east*

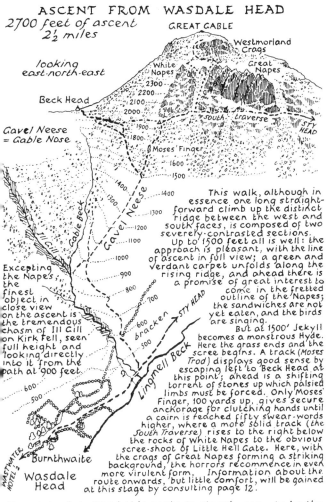

GREAT GABLE

Westmorland
Crags

White
Napes

Great
Napes

Beck Head

south · traverse

STY
HEAD

Gavel Neese
= Gable Nose

β Moses' Finger

This walk, although in essence one long straight-forward climb up the distinct ridge between the west and south faces, is composed of two severely-contrasted sections.

Up to 1500 feet all is well: the approach is pleasant, with the line of ascent in full view; a green and verdant carpet unfolds along the rising ridge, and ahead there is a promise of great interest to come in the fretted outline of the Napes; the sandwiches are not yet eaten, and the birds are singing.

But at 1500' Jekyll becomes a monstrous Hyde. Here the grass ends and the scree begins. A track (*Moses Trod*) displays good sense by escaping left to Beck Head at this point; ahead is a shifting torrent of stones up which palsied limbs must be forced. Only Moses' Finger, 100 yards up, gives secure anchorage for clutching hands until a cairn is reached fifty swear-words higher, where a more solid track (*the South Traverse*) rises to the right below the rocks of White Napes to the obvious scree-shoot of Little Hell Gate. Here, with the crags of Great Napes forming a striking background, the horrors recommence in even more virulent form. Information about the route onwards, but little comfort, will be gained at this stage by consulting page 12.

Excepting the Napes, the finest object in close view on the ascent is the tremendous chasm of Ill Gill on Kirk Fell, seen full height and looking directly into it from the path at 900 feet.

Burnthwaite

Wasdale Head

From Wasdale Head this route is clearly seen to be the most direct way to the summit. It is also the most strenuous. (Its conquest is more wisely announced at supper, afterwards, than at breakfast, in advance).

THE SUMMIT

Great Gable's summit is held in special respect by the older generation of fellwalkers, because here, set in the rocks that bear the top cairn, is the bronze War Memorial tablet of the Fell and Rock Climbing Club, dedicated in 1924, and ever since the inspiring scene of an annual Remembrance Service in November. It is a fitting place to pay homage to men who once loved to walk on these hills and gave their lives defending the right of others to enjoy the same happy freedom for the ultimate crest of Gable is truly characteristic of the best of mountain Lakeland: a rugged crown of rock and boulders and stones in chaotic profusion, a desert without life, a harsh and desolate peak thrust high in the sky above the profound depths all around.

Gable, tough and strong all through its height, has here made a final gesture by providing an outcrop of rock even in its last inches, so that one must climb to touch the cairn (which, being hallowed as a shrine by fellwalkers everywhere, let no man tear asunder lest a thousand curses accompany his guilty flight!). On three sides the slopes fall away immediately, but to the north there extends a small plateau, with a little vegetation, before the summit collapses in the sheer plunge of Gable Crag. The rim of this precipice, and also the top of Westmorland Crags to the south, should be visited for their superlative views.

There are few days in the year when no visitors arrive on the summit. Snow and ice and severe gales may defy those who aspire to reach it in winter, but in the summer months there is a constant parade of perspiring pedestrians across the top from early morning to late evening.

To many fellwalkers this untidy bit of ground is Mecca.

continued

THE SUMMIT

continued

DESCENTS : All ways off the summit are paved with loose stones and continue so for most of the descent.   Allied to roughness is steepness, particularly on the Wasdale side, and care is needed to avoid involuntary slips.   In places, where scree-runners have bared the underlying ground, surfaces are slippery and unpleasant. Never descend Gable in a mad rush!

In fine weather there should be no trouble in distinguishing the various cairned routes ; in mist their direction is identified by the memorial tablet, which faces north overlooking the path to Windy Gap. Not all cairns can be relied upon ; some are not route-markers but indicators of viewpoints and rock-climbs. Generally, however, the principal traffic routes are well-blazed by boots.

In bad conditions the safest line is down the breast of the mountain to Sty Head. Care is needed in locating the descent to Beck Head, which keeps closely to the angle of the north and west faces and does not follow any of the inviting scree-runs on the west side, which end in fields of boulders.   Caution is also advised in attempting direct descents of the Wasdale face if the topography of the Napes is not already familiar.

WINDY GAP

N

BECK HEAD

Gable Crag

2800

2900

summit

2700

2700

2600

STY HEAD

2900

2800

2500

Westmorland Cairn

Westmorland Crags

White Napes

2500

2400

2300

2200

Great Napes

A   B

PLAN OF THE
SUMMIT
AND ENVIRONS

100 Yards

A : Little Hell Gate
B : Great Hell Gate

THE VIEW

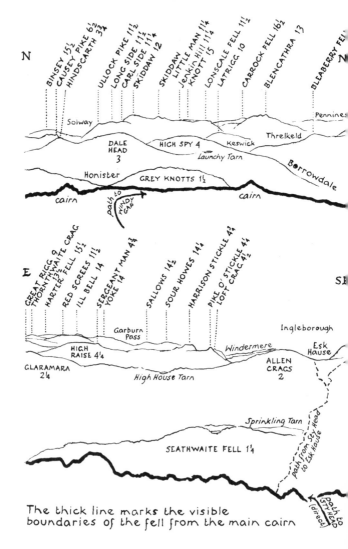

N

BINSEY 15½
CAUSEY PIKE 6½
HINDSCARTH 3¾*
ULLOCK PIKE 11½
LONG SIDE 11½
CARL SIDE 11½*
SKIDDAW 12
SKIDDAW
LITTLE MAN 11¼
Jenkin Hill 11¼
KNOTT 15
LONSCALE FELL 11½
LATRIGG 10
CARROCK FELL 16½
BLENCATHRA 13
BLEABERRY FELL

N

Solway
Pennines
DALE HEAD 3
HIGH SPY 4
Threlkeld
Keswick
Launchy Tarn
Honister
GREY KNOTTS 1½
Borrowdale
cairn
path to WINDY GAP
cairn

E

GREAT RIGG 9
THORNTHWAITE CRAG
HARTER FELL 13½
RED SCREES 15½
ILL BELL 14
SERGEANT MAN 4¾
YOKE 14
SALLOWS 14½
SOUR HOWES 14¼
HARRISON STICKLE 4½
PIKE O' STICKLE 4½
LOFT CRAG 4½

SE

Garburn Pass
Ingleborough
HIGH RAISE 4¼
Windermere
Esk Hause
GLARAMARA 2¼
High House Tarn
ALLEN CRAGS 2
Sprinkling Tarn
SEATHWAITE FELL 1¼
path from Sty Head to Esk House
path to STY HEAD (direct)

The thick line marks the visible
boundaries of the fell from the main cairn

THE VIEW

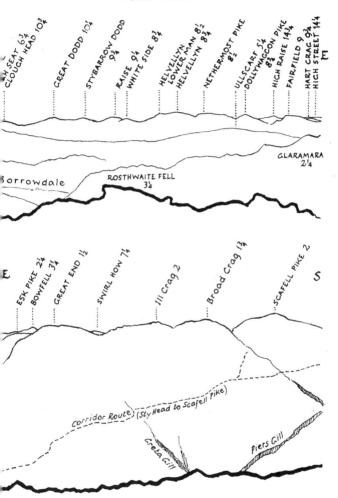

CH SEAT 6¾
CLOUGH HEAD 10¾
GREAT DODD 10¼
STYBARROW DODD 9¾
RAISE 9¼
WHITE SIDE 8¾
HELVELLYN
LOWER MAN 8½
HELVELLYN 8¾
NETHERMOST PIKE 8½
ULLSCARF 5¼
DOLLYWAGGON PIKE 8¾
HIGH RAISE 14¾
FAIRFIELD 9
HART CRAG 9¼
HIGH STREET 14¼

E

GLARAMARA 2¼

Borrowdale

ROSTHWAITE FELL 3¼

E

ESK PIKE 2¼
BOWFELL 3¼
GREAT END 1½
SWIRL HOW 7¼
ILL CRAG 2
BROAD CRAG 1¾
SCAFELL PIKE 2

S

Corridor Route (Sty Head to Scafell Pike)

Greta Gill

Piers Gill

he figures accompanying the names of fells indicate distances in miles

THE VIEW

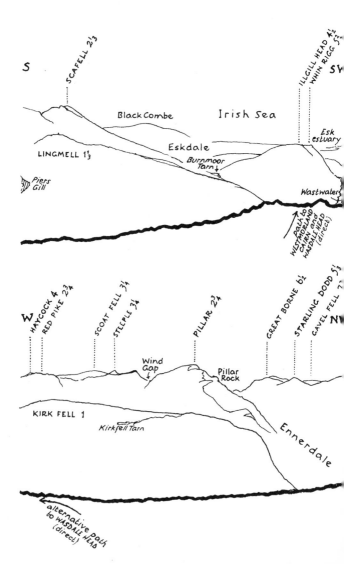

S

SCAFELL 2⅓

Black Combe

Irish Sea

Eskdale

Esk estuary

LINGMELL 1⅓

Burnmoor Tarn ↓

Piers Gill

Wastwater

ILLGILL HEAD 4½

WHIN RIGG 5¼

SW

Wastwater

path to WESTMORLAND CAIRN and WASDALE HEAD (direct)

W

HAYCOCK 4

RED PIKE 2¾

SCOAT FELL 3¼

STEEPLE 3¼

PILLAR 2¾

GREAT BORNE 6½

STARLING DODD 5⅓

GAVEL 7½

NW

Wind Gap ↓

Pillar Rock

KIRK FELL 1

Kirkfell Tarn

Ennerdale

alternative path to WASDALE HEAD (direct)

THE VIEW

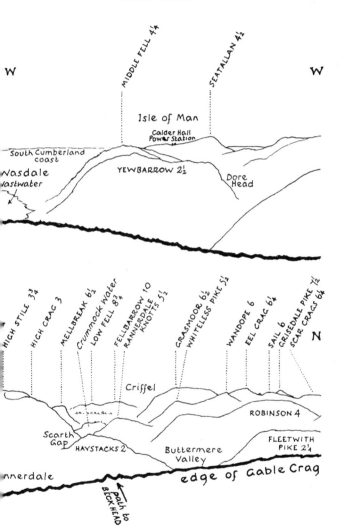

RIDGE ROUTES

TO GREEN GABLE, 2603': NNE, then E and NNE: ½ mile
Depression (Windy Gap) at 2460'
150 feet of ascent
Rough and stony all the way

The best that can be said for the path
is that it is clearly defined throughout,
which is as well, there being unseen
precipices in the vicinity. One section,
where Gable Crag is rounded to reach
Windy Gap, is particularly objectionable
and needs care on smooth rocky steps.

TO KIRK FELL, 2630': NW, then W and SW: 1⅓ miles
Depression (Beck Head) at 2040'   700 feet of ascent

A passing from the sublime to the less sublime, better done the other way.
Pick a way carefully down the north-west ridge, avoiding false
trails that lead only to boulder slopes and keeping generally near
the angle of the ridge, where the footing is firmest. When a line
of fence posts is joined, the remainder of the route is assured,
the posts leading across the depression of Beck Head up the steep
facing slope of Rib End, and visiting first the lower and then the top
summit of Kirk Fell across a wide grassy plateau.

A place to remember.......

Some quite ordinary patches of fellside have
extraordinary significance when they indicate
important route junctions occurring in rough
terrain and not clearly defined by paths
on the ground. The best example is the
upper exit of Lords Rake on Scafell,
and there are many others.

*Illustrated here is
the place where the
North Traverse leaves
the northwest ridge to
cross below Gable
Crag to Windy Gap.*

*Pass between the two cairn
and the track comes into vie*

Westmorland Cairn

Erected in 1876 by two brothers of the name of Westmorland to mark what they considered to be the finest mountain viewpoint in the district, this soundly-built and tidy cairn is wellknown to climbers and walkers alike, and has always been respected. The cairn has maintained its original form throughout the years quite remarkably: apart from visitors who like to add a pebble, it has suffered neither from the weather nor from human despoilers. It stands on the extreme brink of the south face, above steep crags, and overlooks Wasdale. Rocky platforms around make the place ideal for a halt after climbing Great Gable. The cairn is not in sight from the summit but is soon reached by walking 150 yards across the stony top in the direction of Wastwater.

the highest of the
Langdale Pikes

HIGH RAISE ▲

PIKE O' ▲ ▲ HARRISON
STICKLE   STICKLE
LOFT CRAG ● New
Old Hotel ●   ● Hotel
Dungeon Ghyll

MILES
0   1   2   3

from Great Langdale Beck

NATURAL FEATURES

No mountain profile in Lakeland arrests and excites the attention more than that of the Langdale Pikes and no mountain group better illustrates the dramatic appeal of a sudden rising of the vertical from the horizontal; the full height from valley to summit is revealed at a glance in one simple abrupt upsurge to all travellers on the distant shore of Windermere and, more intimately, on the beautiful approach along Great Langdale. Nor is the appeal visual only: that steep ladder to heaven stirs the imagination, and even the emotions, and this is especially so whenever the towering peaks come into view suddenly and unexpectedly. The difference in altitude between top and base is little more than 2000 feet, yet, because it occurs in a distance laterally of only three-quarters of a mile, it is enough to convey a remarkable impression of remoteness, of inaccessibility, to the craggy summits surmounting the rugged slopes.

continued

NATURAL FEATURES

continued

Of the group of peaks known collectively as Langdale Pikes, the highest is Harrison Stickle, and this is the fell that presents such a bold front to, and dominates the middle curve of the valley. It is severed from its satellites westwards by the deep gloomy ravines of Dungeon Ghyll, which, at a lower altitude and near its famous waterfall, turns across the bottom slopes towards Mill Gill, the eastern boundary, so that the fell's actual footing in the valley is quite small, only the width of a field. The ridged summit is liberally buttressed by crags, as is a curious shoulder running down to the hanging valley occupied by Stickle Tarn a considerable sheet of water no less attractive for being partly artificial.

The uninitiated climber who scales Harrison Stickle from Langdale expecting to find the northerly slopes descending as steeply as those he has just ascended will be surprised to see, on reaching the main cairn, that higher ground continues beyond a very shallow depression. The Pikes are, in fact, no more than the abrupt termination of a wide ridge coming down from High Raise, and on this side their aspect, in contrast, is one of almost comical insignificance. But let nothing derogatory be said of Harrison Stickle. The majesty and masculine strength of the Langdale front is itself quite enough to establish the fell as a firm favourite with all, even with those admirers who are content to stand on the road below and gape upwards, while for those who set forth to conquer, it provides a very worthy climb indeed.

looking north-west

1 : The summit
2 : Ridge continuing to
   Thunacar Knott and High Raise
3 : Pike How   4 : Miller Crag
5 : Stickle Tarn 6 : Mill Gill
7 : Dungeon Ghyll
8 : Dungeon Ghyll Force
9 : Great Langdale Beck

The Ravines
of
Dungeon Ghyll

The upper ravine
      between Thorn Crag
      and Harrison Stickle

The middle ravine. The waterfall (on the right), which terminates his section, falls into a rock basin and escapes over a breach in he lip to form a second fall — a most charming scene, revealed nly by a close visit (which entails some scrambling).

The lower ravine

Hidden amongst the trees s Dungeon Ghyll Force, a much-frequented waterfall that does not compare, as an object of beauty, with the little-frequented one mentioned above).

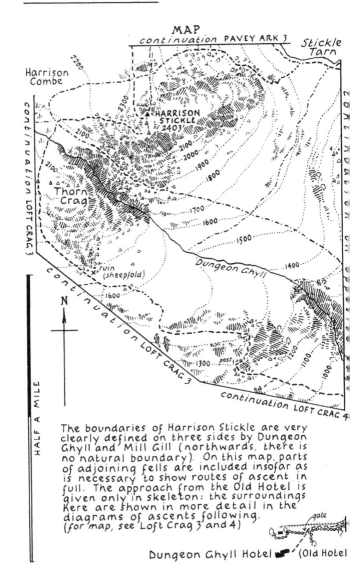

Stickle Tarn

Harrison Combe

continuation LOFT CRAG 3

2200

2100

2100

2100

▲ HARRISON
STICKLE
2403

Thorn Crag

2100

2000

1900

1800

1700

1600

1500

1400

Dungeon Ghyll

ruin
(sheepfold)

1600

continuation LOFT CRAG 3

N

HALF A MILE

1300

post

1200

1100

1000

continuation LOFT CRAG 4

The boundaries of Harrison Stickle are very
clearly defined on three sides by Dungeon
Ghyll and Mill Gill (northwards, there is
no natural boundary). On this map, parts
of adjoining fells are included insofar as
is necessary to show routes of ascent in
full. The approach from the Old Hotel is
given only in skeleton: the surroundings
here are shown in more detail in the
diagrams of ascents following.
(for map, see Loft Crag 3 and 4)

gate

Dungeon Ghyll Hotel ■ (Old Hotel

MAP

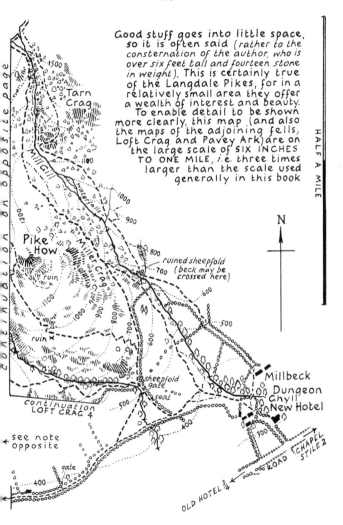

Good stuff goes into little space, so it is often said (rather to the consternation of the author, who is over six feet tall and fourteen stone in weight). This is certainly true of the Langdale Pikes, for in a relatively small area they offer a wealth of interest and beauty. To enable detail to be shown more clearly, this map (and also the maps of the adjoining fells, Loft Crag and Pavey Ark) are on the large scale of SIX INCHES TO ONE MILE, i.e. three times larger than the scale used generally in this book

HALF A MILE

N

Tarn Crag

Pike How

ruin

ruin ×

waterfalls

ruined sheepfold (beck may be crossed here)

sheepfold gate

seat

Millbeck Dungeon Ghyll New Hotel

continuation LOFT CRAG 4

← see note opposite

gate

OLD HOTEL ¾

ROAD

CHAPEL STILE 2

continuation on opposite page

ASCENT FROM DUNGEON GHYLL
ROUTE 1 : via THORN CRAG
2150 feet of ascent : 2 miles

THUNACAR KNOTT

HARRISON STICKLE

Harrison Combe

grass

PIKE O' STICKLE

LOFT CRAG

2100

Thorn Crag

ROUTES 2 and 3

2000
1900
1800
1700

x sheepfold (ruins)

GIMMER CRAG
(a worth-while
short detour on a
level and easy path)

1600 grassy plateau

Dungeon Ghyll

summit
fully in view

1500

view down
Middlefell Gully
to Old Hotel

1400

post

1300

1200
1100
1000
900
800

post

bracken

1100

ROUTE 2

Pike How

bracken

Middlefell
Buttress

summit comes into view

Raven Crag

900

Dungeon Ghyll Force

ROUTES 3 and 4

Dungeon
Ghyll Hotel
(Old Hotel)→

gate

gate

500

gate and sheepfold

seat

ROUTE 4

looking
north-west

ROAD

400

Dungeon
Ghyll
New Hotel

double
bridge

300

Great Langdale Beck

CHAPEL
STILE 2

This is the usual route,
very popular one, and ever
turn and twist of the ingeniou
and circuitous path has bee
faithfully followed by man
generations of walkers. I
is full of interest until the
plateau below Thorn Crag
is reached; thereafter, les.
so. It is rather remarkable
that this route should have
won preference over that via
Pike How (Route 3), which is
direct, much quicker, easie
and better underfoot, whil
being no less attractive.

The similarity in
the names of the
two hotels is a source
of confusion. The *Dungeon
Ghyll Hotel,* three-quarters
of a mile higher in the valley
than the *New Hotel, Dungeon Ghyll*
is now commonly, but not quite correctly,
referred to as the *Old Hotel* (or, amongst the
climbing fraternity, as 'Sid Cross's place').

ASCENT FROM DUNGEON GHYLL
ROUTE 2 : *via* THE DUNGEON GHYLL RAVINES
2150 feet of ascent : 1¾ miles

HARRISON STICKLE

THUNACAR KNOTT

Harrison Combe

PIKE O' STICKLE

grass

2100

ROUTE 1

Fourth Obstacle — a waterslide (insurmountable) between narrow rock walls. *There is no escape from the ravine at this point.* Retreat 150 yards to easier slope; or avoid ravine entirely by slanting across to join Route 3 lower down. *The walls of this final ravine are dirty, loose, in an advanced state of decay, and unsafe. The ravine is subject to bombardment by scree spilling into it from the steep loose slope above; indeed, there is a risk of being brained by a shower of axes.* (See notes for Route 3)

This is an adventurous route, unfrequented and pathless in the ravines, and involving some easy but steep scrambling in impressive surroundings.

1700   grass   → STICKLE TARN

ROUTE 3

1500

1400

This waterfall almost unknown and rarely seen, is certainly one of the most attractive in Lakeland.

Third Obstacle — a beautiful 50' waterfall ends the ravine. Exit up steep rib (or gully) on left

Second Obstacle — a choke of big boulders (shelter) through which, by trial and error, a way may be found free of difficulty.

First Obstacle — a 40' cascade avoided by steep slope on left

1100

ROUTE 2

← summit comes into view

bracken

Middlefell Buttress

Raven Crag

Dungeon Ghyll Hotel (Old Hotel)

gate

800

Dungeon Ghyll Force

ROUTES 3 and 4

gate

500   gate   seat

ROUTE 4

Dungeon Ghyll New Hotel

400

looking north-west

ROAD

300

CHAPEL STILE 2

BOTANISTS! — The sheltered recesses of the ravines harbour many varieties of flowers and ferns and other plants

double bridge

Great Langdale Beck

GHYLL or GILL? Properly GILL, according to the best authorities. GHYLL is a poetical affectation: it is too well established at Dungeon Ghyll to be altered now, and is accepted in a few other cases, e.g. Stock Ghyll, Ambleside.

ASCENT FROM DUNGEON GHYLL
ROUTE 3 : via PIKE HOW
2100 feet of ascent : 1½ miles

HARRISON STICKLE

THUNACAR KNOTT ←

Harrison Combe

grass

PIKE O' STICKLE

ROUTE 1

2100

This steep scree slope abo[ve] the ravine is loose. Exce[pt] for the path, nothing is fir[m]. This is the recently-discovere[d] site of a prehistoric stone-ax[e] 'factory' and much of the scre[e] is the debris from working th[e] stone and not the result of th[e] weathering of the crags abov[e].

Visitors to Langdale who do not know this route are urged to make its acquaintance. It is not only the quickest and easiest way to the top but has two other distinct virtues: first, it is pleasant underfoot, which is more than can be said for many Langdale paths, and, secondly, it is the 'purest' route, being a direct climb which does not encroach upon neighbouring fells.

1800
1700
grass
1600
1500

→ STICKLE TARN

bracken
1200

Pike How –
a splendid viewpoin[t]

1100
ruin
×

Miller Crag

bracken

1000

Middlefell Buttress

Raven Crag

bracken

ruin

bracken

Dungeon Ghyll Hotel (Old Hotel) →

ROUTES 1 and 2

Dungeon Ghyll Force

gate

gate

500
500

600

gate and sheepfold
seat

700

800

ROUTE 4

ROUTE ←

looking north-west

400

Dungeon Ghyll New Hotel

The rough lane along which the path runs from the Old Hotel was the main thoroughfare along the valley before the road was constructed and the hotels opened. A century ago the only place of refreshment hereabouts was Millbeck Farm, and the lane led directly to it from Mickleden. It can still be traced throughout its length bu[t] one of its enclosing walls has been allowed to crumble away.

ROAD

double bridge

Great Langdale Beck

300

← CHAPEL STILE 2

ASCENT FROM DUNGEON GHYLL
ROUTE 4 : *via* STICKLE TARN
2100 feet of ascent :
1¾ miles from the New Hotel ; 2¼ from the Old Hotel

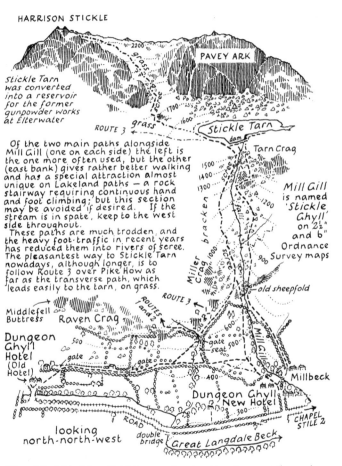

HARRISON STICKLE

PAVEY ARK

Stickle Tarn was converted into a reservoir for the former gunpowder works at Elterwater

ROUTE 3 ← grass

Stickle Tarn

dam

Tarn Crag

Mill Gill is named 'Stickle Ghyll' on 2½" and 6" Ordnance Survey maps

Of the two main paths alongside Mill Gill (one on each side) the left is the one more often used, but the other (east bank) gives rather better walking and has a special attraction almost unique on Lakeland paths — a rock stairway requiring continuous hand and foot climbing ; but this section may be avoided if desired.   If the stream is in spate, keep to the west side throughout.

These paths are much trodden, and the heavy foot-traffic in recent years has reduced them into rivers of scree. The pleasantest way to Stickle Tarn nowadays, although longer, is to follow Route 3 over Pike How as far as the transverse path, which leads easily to the tarn, on grass.

Miller Crag bracken

ROUTE 3 →

old sheepfold

ROUTES 1 and 2

Middlefell Buttress

Raven Crag

Dungeon Ghyll Hotel (Old Hotel)

gate

gate

gate

gate

seat

Mill Gill

Millbeck

Dungeon Ghyll New Hotel

ROAD

looking north-north-west

double bridge

Great Langdale Beck

CHAPEL STILE 2

The highlight of this route is the impressive view of Pavey Ark, one of the finest scenes in Lakeland

ASCENTS FROM BORROWDALE AND GRASMERE

Harrison Stickle is remote from Borrowdale and Grasmere although not too distant to be reached, and the return made in a day's walk.

All *natural* lines of ascent pass over intervening summits.

From BORROWDALE, either (i) first climb High Raise by the Greenup Edge path, or (ii) Pike o' Stickle by way of Langstrath and Stake Pass, in both cases then adopting the ridge routes from those summits. The alternative should be used for return.

From GRASMERE, either (i) first climb Sergeant Man, or (ii) Blea Rigg, descending from the latter to Stickle Tarn, whence the ascent may be completed.

Direct ascents *could* be worked out to avoid traversing other fells, but these would be artificial, probably no easier, and less interesting.

The fells mentioned above have separate chapters in this book, containing diagrams of ascent.

The summit
from
Pike How

The summit
from
Stickle Tarn

THE SUMMIT

The summit is an elevated ridge, 70 yards long and relatively narrow, falling away very sharply in crags at both ends. The main cairn is built on a rocky platform at the northern end and there is another, slightly lower, occupying the southern extremity above the precipitous Langdale face. A scanty covering of turf barely conceals the solid rock that here is very near the surface. The loftiness of the ridge and its commanding position endow a distinction to the summit that might be expected from its noble appearance in distant views.

DESCENTS (to Dungeon Ghyll):
With such a variety of attractive routes available, it would be a pity not to use an alternative to the one adopted for ascent (but Route 2 is less satisfactory as a way down, and needs care). The Pike How route is the easiest (most grass, least scree) and much the quickest. It should be obvious that direct descents from the south cairn are impracticable, but the warning must be given. Similarly, the tempting ridge leading straight down from the top towards Stickle Tarn is defended at its base by an almost continuous wall of crags: a scree gully going down from it on the left side is often used but is unpleasantly loose. Indeed, nothing but hard labour and trouble is to be gained by attempting descents that are independent of the regular paths.

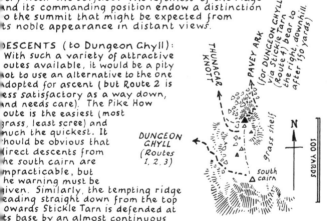

THE VIEW

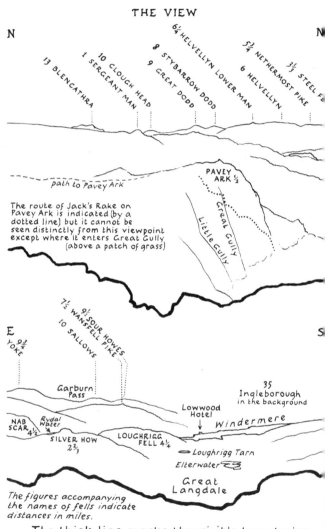

N

N

13 BLENCATHRA

1 SERGEANT MAN

10 CLOUGH HEAD

9 GREAT DODD

8 STYBARROW DODD

6¼ HELVELLYN LOWER MAN

6 HELVELLYN

5¾ NETHERMOST PIKE

3½ STEEL FE

path to Pavey Ark

PAVEY
ARK ½

Great Gully

Little Gully

The route of Jack's Rake on
Pavey Ark is indicated (by a
dotted line) but it cannot be
seen distinctly from this viewpoint
except where it enters Great Gully
(above a patch of grass)

E

S

9¾ YOKE

7½ SOUR HOWES

9½ WANSFELL PIKE

10 SALLOWS

Garburn
Pass

35
Ingleborough
in the background

Lowwood
Hotel

Windermere

NAB
SCAR 4½

Rydal
Water

SILVER HOW
2⅔

LOUGHRIGG
FELL 4¼

← *Loughrigg Tarn*

Elterwater

Great
Langdale

*The figures accompanying
the names of fells indicate
distances in miles.*

The thick line marks the visible boundaries
of the summit from the main cairn

THE VIEW

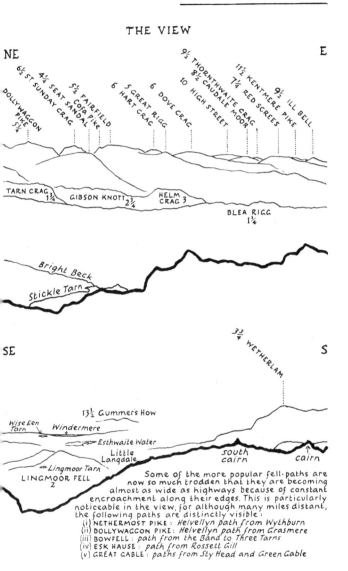

NE   E

DOLLYWAGGON PIKE 5¼
ST SUNDAY CRAG 6½
SEAT SANDAL 4¼
COFA PIKE 5½
FAIRFIELD
HART CRAG 6
GREAT RIGG 5
DOVE CRAG 6
HIGH STREET 10
CAUDALE MOOR 8½
THORNTHWAITE CRAG 9½
RED SCREES 7¼
KENTMERE PIKE 11½
ILL BELL 9½

TARN CRAG 1¾
GIBSON KNOTT 2¼
HELM CRAG 3
BLEA RIGG 1¼

Bright Beck
Stickle Tarn

SE   S

WETHERLAM 3¾

Gummer's How 13½
Wise Een Tarn
Windermere
Esthwaite Water
Little Langdale
south cairn
cairn
Lingmoor Tarn
LINGMOOR FELL 2

Some of the more popular fell-paths are now so much trodden that they are becoming almost as wide as highways because of constant encroachment along their edges. This is particularly noticeable in the view, for although many miles distant, the following paths are distinctly visible:
(i) NETHERMOST PIKE : Helvellyn path from Wythburn
(ii) DOLLYWAGGON PIKE : Helvellyn path from Grasmere
(iii) BOWFELL : path from the Band to Three Tarns
(iv) ESK HAUSE : path from Rossett Gill
(v) GREAT GABLE : paths from Sty Head and Green Gable

THE VIEW

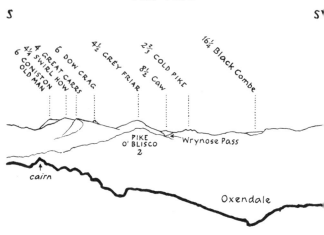

S

SW

6 CONISTON OLD MAN
4½ SWIRL HOW
4 GREAT CARRS
6 DOW CRAG
4½ GREY FRIAR
2⅔ COLD PIKE
8½ CAW
16¼ Black Combe

PIKE O' BLISCO 2

Wrynose Pass

↑ cairn

Oxendale

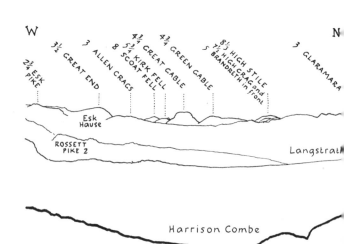

W

N

2¾ ESK PIKE
3½ GREAT END
3 ALLEN CRAGS
8 SCOAT FELL
5¾ KIRK FELL
4¾ GREAT GABLE
4¾ GREEN GABLE
5 BRANDRETH in front
7½ HIGH CRAG 2nd
8½ HIGH STILE
3 GLARAMARA

Esk Hause

ROSSETT PIKE 2

Langstrath

Harrison Combe

THE VIEW

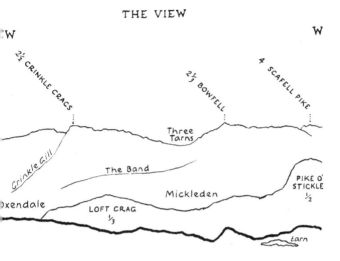

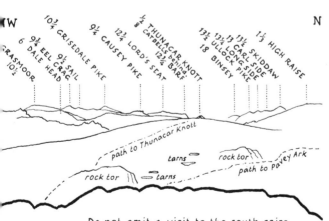

Do not omit a visit to the south cairn, which has a striking downward view of Great Langdale. Stickle Tarn is better seen from here, and Blea Tarn comes into the picture. This is a particularly good viewpoint.

RIDGE ROUTES

To PIKE O' STICKLE, 2323' : ½ mile : W
Depression at 2075' : 250 feet of ascent
An easy walk, ending with an enjoyable scramble

The objective is clearly in view and its distinctive outline is unmistakable. The route is direct (it 'short-cuts' the ridge) and is easily traced in clear weather, although indistinct in marshy ground near the crossing of the stream. The final scramble is steep and rocky, and permits of minor variations.

This is a large-scale map (4" to a mile)

HALF A MILE

To LOFT CRAG, 2270' : ⅓ mile : W, then S and W
Depression at 2070' : 200 feet of ascent
An easy walk, with a fine little summit at the finish

Loft Crag is the biggest eminence on the ridge to the left of Pike o' Stickle. Take the usual route for Langdale (Route 1) turning off right at the Thorn Crag col along a narrow track and then left up a small but prominent scree-run to the ridge.

Harrison Stickle from Loft Crag

RIDGE ROUTES

To THUNACAR KNOTT, 2351' : ½ mile · NNW
Depression at 2225' : 140 feet of ascent
A dull trudge from the spectacular to the uninteresting.

The path starts distinctly from the main cairn but beyond the rock tor becomes obscure in a depression : here follow the line of cairns leading half-left to an improving path (another track develops from a line of cairns going straight on, but loses itself amongst the boulders ahead). The recognised top of Thunacar Knott is marked by a big cairn beyond a tarn, although higher ground is crossed on the way to it. The path keeps to the right and goes on to High Raise.

To PAVEY ARK, 2288'
½ mile : N. then NE
Depression at 2225'
100 feet of ascent
An interesting path

Although not strictly a ridge route, this is a popular walk. From the main cairn, descend the steep but easy rocks directly below to join a good path, much of it over bare rock, linking the two summits. Anyone who does not like the look of the initial descent may avoid it by taking the Thunacar Knott route at the start and slanting across to the Pavey Ark path over grass on the near side of the rock tor.

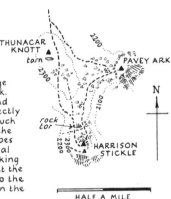

THUNACAR KNOTT
tarn
PAVEY ARK
rock tor
HARRISON STICKLE
N
HALF A MILE

Pavey Ark from the path

top of Jack's Rake

pinnacle

Haystacks

properly
Hay Stacks
(two words)
as on
Ordnance maps

from Gamlin End, High Crag

Gatesgarth
●
HIGH
CRAG ▲

HAYSTACKS
▲

Black ● Sail Y.H.
MILES
0   1   2

NATURAL FEATURES

Haystacks stands unabashed and unashamed in the midst of a circle of much loftier fells, like a shaggy terrier in the company of foxhounds, some of them known internationally, but not one of this distinguished group of mountains around Ennerdale and Buttermere can show a greater variety and a more fascinating arrangement of interesting features. Here are sharp peaks in profusion, tarns with islands and tarns without islands, crags, screes, rocks for climbing and rocks not for climbing, heather tracts, marshes, serpentine trails, tarns with streams and tarns with no streams. All these, with a background of magnificent landscapes, await every visitor to Haystacks but they will be appreciated most by those who go there to linger and explore. It is a place of surprises around corners, and there are many corners. For a man trying to get a persistent worry out of his mind, the top of Haystacks is a wonderful cure.

The fell rises between the deep hollow of Warnscale Bottom near Gatesgarth, and Ennerdale: between a valley familiar to summer motorists and a valley reached only on foot. It is bounded on the west by Scarth Gap, a pass linking the two. The Buttermere aspect is the better known, although this side is often dark in shadow and seen only as a silhouette against the sky: here, above Warnscale, is a great wall of crags. The Ennerdale flank, open to the sun, is friendlier but steep and rough nevertheless.

Eastwards, beyond the tangle of tors and outcrops forming the boundary of Haystacks on this side, a broad grass slope rises easily and unattractively to Brandreth on the edge of the Borrowdale watershed; beyond is Derwent country.

The spelling of Haystacks as one word is a personal preference of the author (and others), and probably arises from a belief that the name originated from the resemblance of the scattered tors on the summit to stacks of hay in a field. If this were so, the one word *Haystacks* would be correct (as it is in *Haycock*).
But learned authorities state that the name derives from the Icelandic 'stack', meaning 'a columnar rock', and that the true interpretation is *High Rocks*. This is logical and appropriate. *High Rocks* is a name of two words and would be wrongly written as *Highrocks*.

The summit tarn

Big Stack,
looking east from a point
near the path to the
summit from
Scarth Gap.

In the picture below
Big Stack appears on
the extreme right.

The north crags,
looking west from the
slopes of Green Crag.

The path is seen
skirting the cliff
on the left

MAP

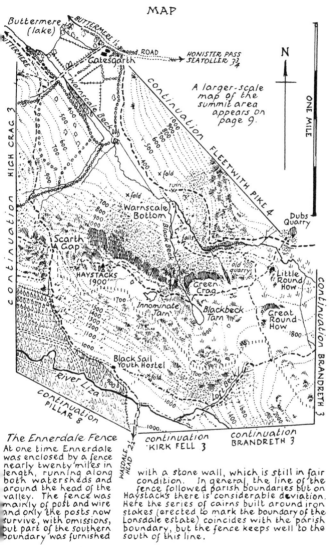

The Ennerdale Fence

At one time Ennerdale was enclosed by a fence nearly twenty miles in length, running along both watersheds and around the head of the valley. The fence was mainly of post and wire and only the posts now survive, with omissions, but part of the southern boundary was furnished with a stone wall, which is still in fair condition. In general, the line of the fence followed parish boundaries but on Haystacks there is considerable deviation. Here the series of cairns built around iron stakes (erected to mark the boundary of the Lonsdale estate) coincides with the parish boundary, but the fence keeps well to the south of this line.

A larger-scale map of the summit area appears on page 9.

ASCENT FROM GATESGARTH
1550 feet of ascent : 1¼ miles

via SCARTH GAP   HAYSTACKS

Big Stack

Stack Rake

Scarth Gap

From Scarth Gap take a thin track slanting up to the right until a long fan of scree is reached. Go up this to a recess: rocky exit on the left

HIGH CRAG

1500 HIGH CRAG

1300

1200

1100

gap

High Wax Knott

Low Wax Knott

It is a test of iron discipline to pass without halting several large comfortable boulders athwart the path.

1000

700

600

500

400

900

800

bracken

Scarth Gap is one of the pleasantest of the foot-passes. Apart from the steep section above the sheepfold, the gradients are gentle and the views both ahead and behind are full of interest. The path is generally good, but it is significant that the roughest places are those where the original zigzags have been butchered by 'short-cutters'

Coupled with a return by the Warnscale route to make a full 'round' journey the ascent of Haystacks via the pass of Scarth Gap is a prelude of much merit and beauty to a mountain walk of unique character, the whole distance being no more than five miles. Save it, however, for a fine clear day.

Leave Gatesgarth by the sheep-pens, at a signpost to Scarth Gap

Gatesgarth

sheepfold

BUTTERMERE via BURTNESS WOOD

ROAD

Buttermere

looking south

ASCENT FROM GATESGARTH
via WARNSCALE

1600 feet of ascent : 2¾ miles

HAYSTACKS

Green Crag

dead trees

old quarry

DUBS

F
E
D

1200
1100
1000
900
800
700
600
500

C B A

1100
1000

DUBS QUARRY and HONISTER PASS

ravine

falls

fall

FLEETWITH PIKE rises steeply on this side

quarry road (not used on this ascent)

ruin

Warnscale Beck

Slack Gill
bracken

A : Slack Gill
B : Warn Gill
C : The Y Gully
D : Toreador Gully
E : Green Crag Gully
F : Little Round How
G : Great Round How
H : Blackbeck Tarn
I : Innominate Tarn

Warnscale Bottom

x circular sheepfold

x old fold

Cross the stream near the confluence (easier said than done). Try a little higher where it runs in two channels.

looking south

artificial cut   excellent via a

Two paths climb out of Warnscale Bottom. On the left, in a great loop, rises a wellknown quarry road (this is an excellent route to Honister). On the right, across the beck, is an old 'made' path, originally serving a quarry : this is now little used but is still well-cairned, and it provides a fascinating stairway of zigs and zags over rough ground with impressive views of the wall of crags above : this is the path to take. (It is possible to scramble up the right may be taken : this skirts the alongside Black Beck, but this is not recommended).

The grassy upland is reached directly opposite Great Round How, the path at this point being joined by another from Dubs Quarry. Full of variety and interesting situations, it swings right, passing Blackbeck and Innominate Tarns, to the top of the fell. Or, before reaching Innominate Tarn, a track on he right may be taken : this skirts the rim of the crags and crowds more thrills into the walk.

Gatesgarth used to be served by buses, but isn't now.

easy level walking

Gatesgarth

SCARTH GAP

BUTTERMERE 1½

HONISTER PASS SEATOLLER 3¾   ROAD

Gatesgarthdale Beck

For sustained interest, impressive crag scenery, beautiful views, and a most delightful arrangement of tarns and rocky peaks, this short mountain excursion ranks with the very best.

ASCENT FROM HONISTER PASS
1050 feet of ascent : 2¼ miles

A note of explanation is required.   This ascent-route does not conform to the usual pattern, being more in the nature of an upland cross-country walk than a mountain climb : there are two pronounced descents before foot is set on Haystacks. The wide variety of scene and the fascinating intricacies of the path are justification for the inclusion of the route in this book.

HAYSTACKS

If returning to Honister, note the path to Brandreth just below Innominate Tarn. By using this until it joins the Great Gable path and then swinging left around Dubs Bottom, the Drum House can be regained without extra effort or time.

After traversing the back of Green Crag the path drops to the outlet of Blackbeck Tarn, rising stonily therefrom with a profound abyss on the right. This section is the highlight of the walk. An alternative way to the top, turning off opposite the Brandreth junction, follows closely the edge of the crags.

tarn
1800
Innominate Tarn
BRANDRETH
Blackbeck Tarn
Green Crag
Great Round How
1600
Little Round How
grass
WARNSCALE BOTTOM
1500
1400
Dubs Bottom
1500
WARNSCALE BOTTOM
1600
Dubs Quarry (disused)

looking west

BRANDRETH GREAT GABLE
1700
foundations of Drum House
1700
1600
Old tramway
1500
1400
rock cutting
1300
1200
quarry road
quarry buildings
Honister Pass 1190'
BUTTERMERE

From the hut at Dubs Quarry leave the path and go down to the stream, crossing it (somehow) where its silent meanderings through the Dub marshes assume a noisy urgency.

From the top of Honister Pass Haystacks is nowhere in sight, and even when it comes into view, after crossing the shoulder of Fleetwith Pike at the Drum House, it is insignificant against the towering background of Pillar, being little higher in altitude and seemingly remote across the wide depression of Dubs Bottom. But, although the route here described is not a natural approach, the elevation of Honister Pass, its car-parking facilities and the unerring pointer of the tramway make access to Haystacks particularly convenient from this point!

ASCENT FROM ENNERDALE
(BLACK SAIL YOUTH HOSTEL)

970 feet of ascent
1¼ miles

HAYSTACKS

tarn   tarn   1800
                1700
Scarth   1600
Gap   1500

1500

grass

1300

GREAT GABLE   KIRK FELL

1200

An alternative is to use the path to Honister by way of Loft Beck as far as the Brandreth fence, where turn left to reach the summit from the east.

1100

looking south-east from Scarth Gap

grass

1000

GILLERTHWAITE ←

Black Sail Youth Hostel

looking north

This route is likely to be of interest only to youth hostellers staying at the magnificently situated Black Sail Hut. Other mortals, denied this privilege, cannot conveniently use Ennerdale Head as a starting point for mountain ascents.

formerly a shepherd's hut, ...

Black Sail Youth Hostel

THE SUMMIT

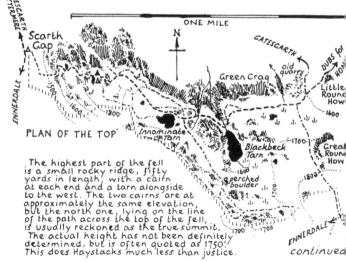

ONE MILE

N

PLAN OF THE TOP

. The highest part of the fell
is a small rocky ridge, fifty
yards in length, with a cairn
at each end and a tarn alongside
to the west. The two cairns are at
approximately the same elevation,
but the north one, lying on the line
of the path across the top of the fell,
is usually reckoned as the true summit.
 The actual height has not been definitely
determined, but is often quoted as 1750!
This does Haystacks much less than justice.

continued

THE SUMMIT

continued

Haystacks fails to qualify for inclusion in the author's "best half-dozen" only because of inferior height, a deficiency in vertical measurement. Another thousand feet would have made all the difference.

But for beauty, variety and interesting detail, for sheer fascination and unique individuality, the summit-area of Haystacks is supreme. This is in fact the best fell-top of all — a place of great charm and fairyland attractiveness. Seen from a distance, these qualities are not suspected: indeed, on the contrary, the appearance of Haystacks is almost repellent when viewed from the higher surrounding peaks: black are its bones and black is its flesh. With its thick covering of heather it is dark and sombre even when the sun sparkles the waters of its many tarns, gloomy and mysterious even under a blue sky. There are fierce crags and rough screes and outcrops that will be grittier still when the author's ashes are scattered here.

Yet the combination of features, of tarn and tor, of cliff and cove, the labyrinth of corners and recesses, the maze of old sheepwalks and paths, form a design, or a lack of design, of singular appeal and absorbing interest. One can forget even a raging toothache on Haystacks.

perched boulder on a rock platform

Note the profile in shadow. Some women have faces like that.

On a first visit, learn thoroughly the details of the mile-long main path across the top, a magnificent traverse, because this serves as the best introduction to the geography of the fell.

Having memorised this, several interesting deviations may be made: the parallel alternative above the rim of the north face, the scramble onto Big Stack, the 'cross-country' route around the basin of Blackbeck Tarn, the walk alongside the fence, and so on.

typical summit tors

DESCENTS: Leave the top of Haystacks only by a recognisable route. It is possible to make rough descents in the vicinity (left bank) of Black Beck and Green Crag gully, but more advisable to regard the whole of the north edge as highly dangerous. The only advice that can be given to a novice lost on Haystacks in mist is that he should kneel down and pray for safe deliverance.

THE VIEW

This is not a case of distance lending enchantment to the view, because apart from a glimpse of Skiddaw above the Robinson-Hindscarth depression and a slice of the Helvellyn range over Honister, the scene is predominantly one of high mountains within a five-mile radius. And really good they look — the enchantment is close at hand. Set in a light surround, they are seen in revealing detail: a rewarding study deserving leisurely appreciation.

Principal Fells

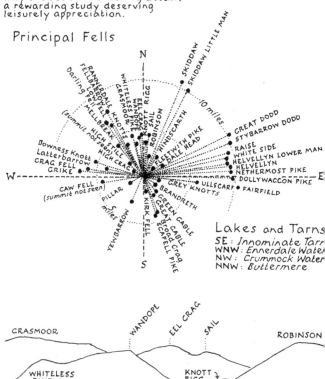

Lakes and Tarns

SE : *Innominate Tarn*
WNW : *Ennerdale Water*
NW : *Crummock Water*
NNW : *Buttermere*

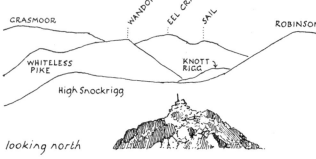

looking north

RIDGE ROUTES

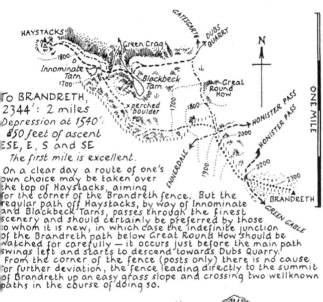

To BRANDRETH, 2344': 2 miles
Depression at 1540'
850 feet of ascent
ESE, E, S and SE

The first mile is excellent.

On a clear day a route of one's own choice may be taken over the top of Haystacks, aiming for the corner of the Brandreth fence. But the regular path off Haystacks, by way of Innominate and Blackbeck Tarns, passes through the finest scenery and should certainly be preferred by those to whom it is new, in which case the indefinite junction of the Brandreth path below Great Round How should be watched for carefully — it occurs just before the main path swings left and starts to descend towards Dubs Quarry.
From the corner of the fence (posts only) there is no cause for further deviation, the fence leading directly to the summit of Brandreth up an easy grass slope and crossing two wellknown paths in the course of doing so.

To HIGH CRAG, 2443'
1¼ miles: W, then NW
Depression at 1425' (Scarth Gap)
1100 feet of ascent
A fine walk in spite of scree

Follow faithfully the thin track trending west from the summit, a delightful game of ins and outs and downs although the scree to which it leads is less pleasant: at the foot slant right to Scarth Gap. More scree is encountered across the pass on the climb to Seat; then a good ridge follows to the final tower of High Crag: this deteriorates badly into slippery scree on the later stages of the ascent.

High Crag, from Scarth Gap

HALF A MILE

Pike o' Stickle

the second of the
Langdale Pikes

Pike OF Stickle,
to be correct

from Gimmer Crag

HIGH RAISE ▲

PIKE O'   ▲ ▲ HARRISON
STICKLE   STICKLE

LOFT CRAG ● New
Old Hotel ●   Hotel
Dungeon Ghyll

MILES
0   1   2   3

NATURAL FEATURES

Simple lines are often the most effective, and the smoothly-soaring pyramid of Pike o' Stickle, rising to a tapering thimble of rock without interruption or halt between valley and summit, is an imposing and impressive feature that contributes much to the grandeur of the head of Great Langdale. The unbroken sweep of Stickle Breast above Mickleden is one of the most continuously steep slopes in the district, rising nearly 2,000 feet over a lateral distance of half a mile. Dry scree gullies sever the craggy upper storey from the neighbouring fellsides, but a lofty ridge connects it with the castellated skyline overlooking Dungeon Ghyll and Langdale. A strong contrast to this battlemented facade is that provided by the dreary upland hollow lying beyond (Harrison Combe) from which easy slopes fall away to Stake Pass, northwest, pausing in their descent to form the broad plateau of Martcrag Moor.

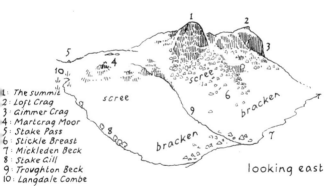

1 : The summit
2 : Loft Crag
3 : Gimmer Crag
4 : Martcrag Moor
5 : Stake Pass
6 : Stickle Breast
7 : Mickleden Beck
8 : Stake Gill
9 : Troughton Beck
10 : Langdale Combe

looking east

Thousands of years ago, before the dawn of history, Pike o' Stickle was the scene of an industry the evidences of which have only recently been discovered, and the fell is now established as the country's most important site of stone-axe manufacture by neolithic man. As such it is attracting increasing attention by archaeologists and geologists, but walkers with no expert knowledge of the subject will also find an absorbing interest in a study of the related literature, as yet incomplete, and they may care to combine with their expeditions in this area a search into the dim but fascinating secrets of the past.

The south scree, from Micklede

The Stone Axe Factory

The intrusion of a narrow vein of a very hard stone in the volcanic rocks of Great Langdale, emerging on the surface along a high-level contour around the head of the valley, provided the material from which the prehistoric natives of the district fashioned their axes. Working sites have been located from Martcrag Moor to Harrison Stickle, but the screes of Pike o' Stickle have yielded the most prolific discoveries, and especially the 'south scree' where hundreds of specimens, originally rejected because of imperfections, have been collected in recent years.

The really remarkable feature is not so much the presence of this particular variety of stone, nor the making of implements from it so long ago; the facts that most tax the imagination are, first, that the primitive inhabitants of Lakeland should have located such an insignificant geological fault and recognised its value, and secondly, that the plentiful evidences of their industry should have remained undisturbed and unnoticed throughout the ages until modern times.

In the rock wall of the south scree is this well-made artificial cave. Its connection with stone-axe manufacture hereabouts has not yet been accepted authoritatively, although the coincidence seems too great to be denied. A few feet square, it provides excellent shelter for several persons.

Length 9½"
Width 3"
Maximum
  Thickness 1½"
Weight 2¼ lbs

Stone axe found on Pike o' Stickle — a particularly good specimen in the collection of Mr. R. G. Plint, of Kendal

MAP

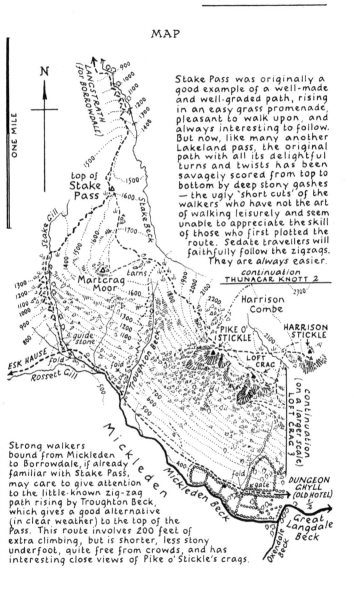

Stake Pass was originally a good example of a well-made and well-graded path, rising in an easy grass promenade, pleasant to walk upon, and always interesting to follow. But now, like many another Lakeland pass, the original path with all its delightful turns and twists has been savagely scored from top to bottom by deep stony gashes — the ugly 'short cuts' of the walkers who have not the art of walking leisurely and seem unable to appreciate the skill of those who first plotted the route. Sedate travellers will faithfully follow the zigzags. They are *always* easier.

continuation THUNACAR KNOTT 2

Strong walkers bound from Mickleden to Borrowdale, if already familiar with Stake Pass, may care to give attention to the little-known zig-zag path rising by Troughton Beck, which gives a good alternative (in clear weather) to the top of the Pass. This route involves 200 feet of extra climbing, but is shorter, less stony underfoot, quite free from crowds, and has interesting close views of Pike o' Stickle's crags.

ASCENT FROM MICKLEDEN
2000 feet of ascent

3¼ miles via Troughton Beck,
1¾ miles direct (from the
Dungeon Ghyll Old Hotel)

PIKE O' STICKLE

cave

TOP OF STAKE PASS

Martcrag Moor

2000

1700   1800

1600

1500

1400

scree-run

bracken

In the final gully the best footing is on the east side

Initially there is no path by the beck, but one materialises as the ground steepens. It is indistinct on top of the fell.

1300

1200

1100

1000

900

800

Troughton Beck

bracken   grass

sheepfold

STAKE PASS and ESK HAUSE

This path in the strip of bracken between scree-runs has obviously been made by travellers descending at speed: it is not 'stepped' and is of little help in ascent.

shallow dry gully

patch of rushes

big boulder

bracken

800

700

600

500

looking north-north-west

400

Mickleden Beck

Mickleden

ruin

gate   DUNGEON GHYLL (OLD HOTEL)

sheepfold

Pike o' Stickle is almost invariably reached from the valley by turning left off the usual Harrison Stickle path at the Thorn Crag col, but illustrated here are two other possibilities —
first, via the unfrequented zig-zags climbing the west bank of Troughton Beck, by which the path coming up from the top of Stake Pass may be joined for the summit of the Pike; *second*, direct up the south scree, a continuously steep and unpleasant scramble in prickly, unstable scree, and of interest only to searchers after stone axes; the route is dry and dusty but bilberries will be found in season higher up and will seem, by the time they are reached, a greater prize than stone axes to the untrained eye and unlearned mind, which will already have selected and discarded hundreds of likely axes in the splintery stones and debris heaps that litter this desperate climb. In a buttoned-up plastic mac, the ascent is purgatory.

ASCENT FROM THE TOP OF STAKE PASS
800 feet of ascent : 1⅓ miles

PIKE O' STICKLE

looking south-east

The surroundings are dull but interest is sustained by the striking sugarloaf appearance of the Pike, which is no less imposing on this unfamiliar side and makes a worthwhile objective.
The summit is a will-o'-the-wisp on this approach, frequently coming into and vanishing from sight in rather amusing fashion.

Evidences of stone-axe manufacture have been discovered in the upland valley of Stake Beck

county boundary

2200
2100
2000
1900
1800
1700

Troughton Beck

tarns

Martcrag Moor

grass

1700

Stake Beck

boulders

moraines

1600

cairn

top of
Stake Pass
1576'

BORROWDALE
(STONETHWAITE 4)

GREAT LANGDALE
(DUNGEON GHYLL
OLD HOTEL 3¼)

By a short detour the cairn on Martcrag Moor may be visited. This rocky little top is a commanding viewpoint for the head of Mickleden and it is wonderfully satisfying to lie here in the sunshine and watch parties struggling up Rossett Gill and Stake Pass from the sheepfold far below. Here, too, is one of the most impressive views of Bowfell.

The summit of Pike o' Stickle from the north-west

The cairn on Martcrag Moor

THE SUMMIT

HARRISON
STICKLE

The summit is the perfect dome suggested by its appearance from a distance, being circular in plan and bell-shaped, with almost precipitous slopes rising up to it on all sides before finally tapering away gently to the highest point. The top is a pleasant green sward of ample proportions, but exploration is severely restricted by the surrounding crags. Access to the cairn is gained by an easy scramble on the more broken northern slope, this being the only side 'open' to walkers.

DESCENTS :

To Great Langdale : Expert scree-runners will come down the open gully immediately east of the summit-dome and reach the valley-bottom in Mickleden in a matter of minutes, but ordinary mortals will find this route very trying to the temper, although it is probably the safest way in mist and the most sheltered in bad weather.   The more usual procedure normally is to join a good path (from Harrison Stickle) at the Thorn Crag col. The route via Troughton Beck has no merits in descent.

1 : top of Stake Pass

ignore these paths, which go nowhere in particular.

2 : Harrison Stickle
3 : Loft Crag ; Thorn Crag
4 : Mickleden (direct)

To Borrowdale : The path to the top of Stake Pass presents no difficulties in clear weather and must be attempted in mist because there is no other ; take care to start on the right track.

RIDGE ROUTE

PIKE O'
STICKLE

HARRISON
STICKLE

THORN
CRAG col
LOFT
CRAG

¼ mile

TO LOFT CRAG, 2270'
⅓ mile : E, then SE
100 feet of ascent

At the first depression, follow the less distinct track branching up right : this keeps an interesting course along the ridge

THE VIEW

The view is extensive, especially to the north, although it is interrupted in other directions by nearby higher ground. But the best thing to be seen is below the skyline: the head of Mickleden far beneath, with Bowfell a magnificent object as a background to the picture.

Principal Fells

N

BINSEY
SKIDDAW
CARL SIDE
LONSCALE FELL
LONG SIDE
KNOTT
BARF
LORD'S SEAT
BLENCATHRA
CAUSEY
GRISEDALE PIKE
CATBELLS
GRANGE FELL
EEL CRAG
BARF PIKE
HIGH SPY
HIGH SEAT
GRASMOOR
DALE HEAD
HIGH RAISE
HELVELLYN LOWER MAN
20 miles
15 miles
10 miles
THUNACAR KNOTT
HELVELLYN
NETHERMOST PIKE
DOLLYWAGGON PIKE
HIGH STILE
BRANDRETH
SERGEANT'S CRAG
CLARAMARA
ST SUNDAY CRAG
GREEN GABLE
PAVEY
FAIRFIELD
GREAT GABLE
PAVEY
HART CRAG
KIRK FELL
GREAT RIGG
DOVE CRAG
HIGH STREET
GREAT END
ESK PIKE
HARRISON STICKLE
THORNTHWAITE CRAG
W--SCAFELL PIKE
SILVER HOW
E
BOWFELL
LOFT CRAG
WANSFELL PIKE
LOUGHRIGG FELL
CRINKLE CRAGS
COLD PIKE
LINGMOOR FELL
GREY FRIAR
GREAT CARRS
SWIRL HOWS
WETHERLAM
5 miles

S

Also prominently seen, but not shown on the diagram for lack of space, is Pike o' Blisco across Mickleden in front of the Coniston Fells

Lakes and Tarns

ESE : *Loughrigg Tarn*
ESE : *Elterwater*
SE : *Windermere (upper reach and strip of middle)*
SE : *Lingmoor Tarn*
SE : *Esthwaite Water*
SSE : *Blea Tarn*
WNW : *Nameless tarns on Martcrag Moor*
NNW : *Tarn at Leaves (on Rosthwaite Fell)*

Pillar

2927'

from Brin Crag, Brandreth

NATURAL FEATURES

Great Gable, Pillar and Steeple are the three mountain names on Lakeland maps most likely to fire the imagination of youthful adventurers planning a first tour of the district, inspiring exciting visions of slim, near-vertical pinnacles towering grandly into the sky.

Great Gable lives up to its name, especially if climbed from Wasdale; Pillar has a fine bold outline but is nothing like a pillar; Steeple is closely overlooked by a higher flat-topped fell and not effectively seen.

Pillar, in fact, far from being a spire of slender proportions, is a rugged mass broadly based on half the length of Ennerdale, a series of craggy buttresses supporting the ridge high above this wild north face; and the summit itself, far from being pointed, is wide and flat. The name of the fell therefore clearly derives from a conspicuous feature on the north face directly below the top, the most handsome crag in Lakeland, originally known as the Pillar Stone and now as Pillar Rock. The Rock, despite a remote and lonely situation, had a well-established local notoriety and fame long before tourists called wider attention to it, and an object of such unique appearance simply had to be given a descriptive name, although, at the time, one was not yet needed to identify the mountain of which it formed part. *The Pillar* was an inspiration of shepherds. Men of letters could not have chosen better.

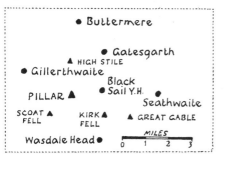

The north face of the fell has a formidable aspect. Crags and shadowed hollows, scree and tumbled boulders, form a wild, chaotic scene, a setting worthy of a fine mountain.

continued

NATURAL FEATURES

continued

Pillar is the highest mountain west of Great Gable from which it is sufficiently removed in distance to exhibit distinctive slopes on all sides. It dominates the sunset area of Lakeland superbly, springing out of the valleys of Mosedale and Ennerdale, steeply on the one side and dramatically on the other, as befits the overlord of the western scene. A narrow neck of land connects with a chain of other grand fells to the south, and a depression forms the east boundary and is crossed by Black Sail Pass at 1800' but elsewhere the full height of the fell from valley level is displayed. Some of the streams flow west via Ennerdale Water and some south via Wast Water, but their fate, discharge into the Irish Sea from the coast near Seascale, is the same, only a few miles separating the two outlets.

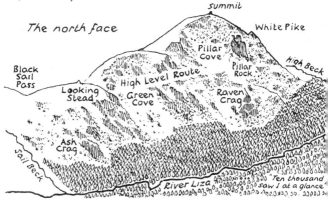

Afforestation in Ennerdale has cloaked the lower slopes on this side in a dark and funereal shroud of foreign trees, an intrusion that nobody who knew Ennerdale of old can ever forgive, the former charm of the valley having been destroyed thereby. We condemn vandalism and sanction this mess! Far better the old desolation of boulder and bog, when a man could see the sky, than this new desolation of regimented timber shutting out the light of day. It is an offence to the eyes to see Pillar's once-colourful fellside now hobbled in such a dowdy and ill-suited skirt, just as it is to see a noble animal caught in a trap. Yet, such is the majesty and power of this fine mountain that it can shrug off the insults and indignities, and its summit soars no less proudly above. It is the admirers of this grand pile who feel the hurt.

A Pillar Rock
portfolio

from the east

Pillar 5

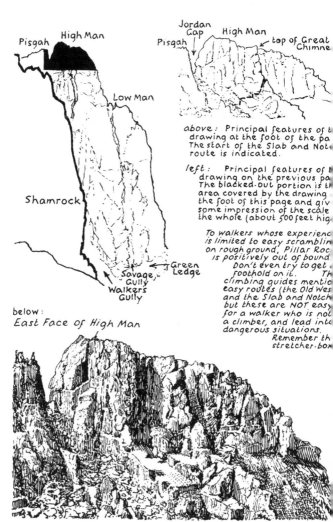

Pisgah — High Man

Jordan Gap — Pisgah — High Man — top of Great Chimney

Low Man

Shamrock

Green Ledge

Savage Gully
Walkers Gully

above: Principal features of the drawing at the foot of the page. The start of the Slab and Notch route is indicated.

left: Principal features of the drawing on the previous page. The blacked-out portion is the area covered by the drawing at the foot of this page and gives some impression of the scale of the whole (about 500 feet high).

To walkers whose experience is limited to easy scrambling on rough ground, Pillar Rock is positively out of bounds. Don't even try to get a foothold on it. The climbing guides mention easy routes (the Old West and the Slab and Notch) but these are NOT easy for a walker who is not a climber, and lead into dangerous situations.
Remember the stretcher-box.

below:
East Face of High Man

as seen from the Shamrock Traverse

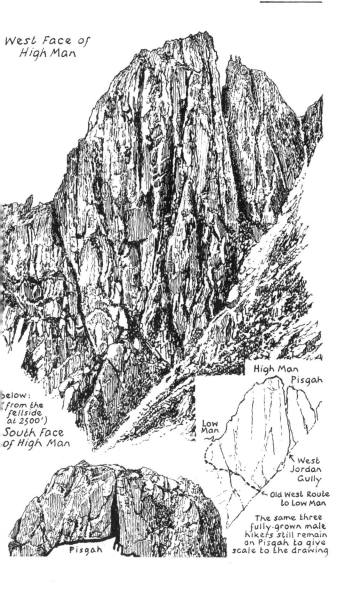

West Face of
High Man

High Man

Pisgah

Low
Man

West
Jordan
Gully

Old West Route
to Low Man

below:
(from the
fellside
at 2500')
South Face
of High Man

Pisgah

The same three
fully-grown male
hikers still remain
on Pisgah to give
scale to the drawing

MAP

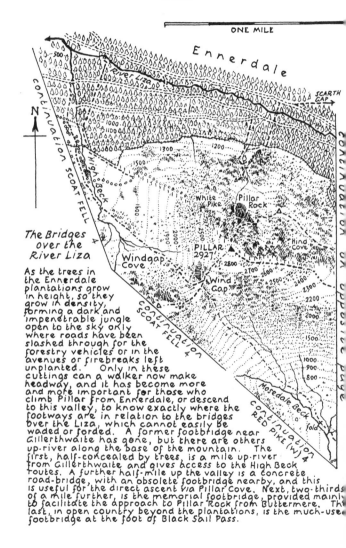

ONE MILE

Ennerdale

River Liza

SCARTH GAP

N

continuation SCOAT FELL 4

High Beck

500
1000
1100
1300
1200
1500
1600
1800
1900
2000

White Pike

Pillar Rock

continuation on opposite page

Hind Cove

PILLAR 2927

2500
2700
2600
2400
2300
2200
2000
1500
1000
900
800

Wind Gap

Windgap Cove

continuation SCOAT FELL 4

Mosedale Beck

continuation RED PIKE (W) 4

fold

The Bridges over the River Liza

As the trees in the Ennerdale plantations grow in height, so they grow in density, forming a dark and impenetrable jungle open to the sky only where roads have been slashed through for the forestry vehicles or in the avenues or firebreaks left unplanted.   Only in these cuttings can a walker now make headway, and it has become more and more important for those who climb Pillar from Ennerdale, or descend to this valley, to know exactly where the footways are in relation to the bridges over the Liza, which cannot easily be waded or forded.   A former footbridge near Gillerthwaite has gone, but there are others up-river along the base of the mountain.   The first, half-concealed by trees, is a mile up-river from Gillerthwaite and gives access to the High Beck routes. A further half-mile up the valley is a concrete road-bridge, with an obsolete footbridge nearby, and this is useful for the direct ascent via Pillar Cove.   Next, two-thirds of a mile further, is the memorial footbridge, provided mainly to facilitate the approach to Pillar Rock from Buttermere. The last, in open country beyond the plantations, is the much-used footbridge at the foot of Black Sail Pass.

MAP

Ennerdale is an inhospitable valley, without refuge on a wet day. It is useful to know that shelter can be found in the flood passage under the road-bridge: in normal conditions this is quite dry.

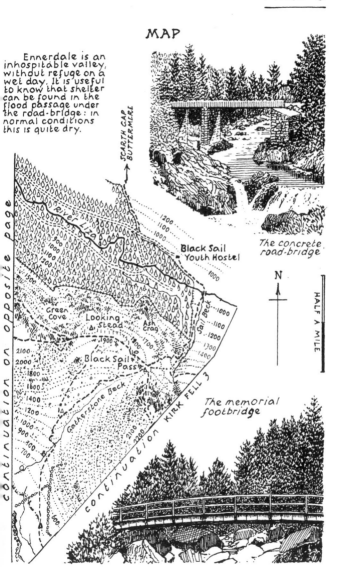

The concrete road-bridge

N

HALF A MILE

The memorial footbridge

continuation on opposite page

continuation KIRK FELL 3

ASCENT FROM WASDALE HEAD
2700 feet of ascent
4½ miles via Black Sail Pass
3¼ miles via Wind Gap

The short cut is not really a time-saver
in ascent, the better plan being to go
on to the top of the Pass and do the
whole ridge.

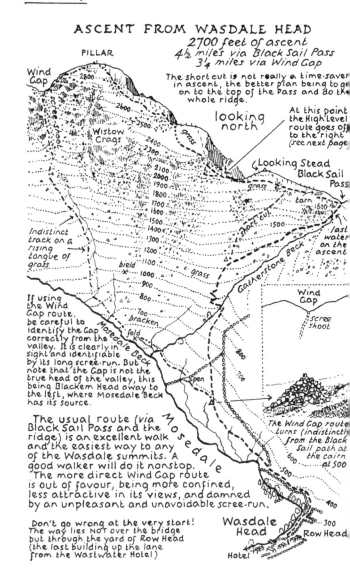

PILLAR

Wind Gap

2800

Wistow Crags

2600
2500
2400
2300
2100
2000
1900
1800
1700
1600
1500
1400
1300
1200
1100
1000
900
800

looking north

grass

At this point
the High Level
route goes off
to the right
(see next page)

Looking Stead
Black Sail Pass

grass

tarn

short cut

1500

last water on the ascent

Gatherstone Beck

Indistinct track on a rising tongue of grass

bield

c. grass

Wind Gap

scree shoot

fold

Mosedale Beck

Too bracken

pen

800

700

If using the Wind Gap route, be careful to identify the Gap correctly from the valley. It is clearly in sight and identifiable by its long scree-run. But note that the Gap is not the true head of the valley, this being Blackem Head away to the left, where Mosedale Beck has its source.

The Wind Gap route turns (indistinctly) from the Black Sail path at the cairn at 500

The usual route (via Black Sail Pass and the ridge) is an excellent walk and the easiest way to any of the Wasdale summits. A good walker will do it nonstop. The more direct Wind Gap route is out of favour, being more confined, less attractive in its views, and damned by an unpleasant and unavoidable scree-run.

Mosedale

600

500

400

Wasdale Head

Row Head

300

Don't go wrong at the very start! The way lies NOT over the bridge but through the yard of Row Head (the last building up the lane from the Wastwater Hotel)

Hotel

ASCENT FROM ENNERDALE
(BLACK SAIL YOUTH HOSTEL)

2000 feet of ascent: 2¾ miles
(2100 feet, 3 miles by High Level Route)

PILLAR

Great Doup

Pillar Rock

stretcher box

Hind Cove

cross

Green Cove

Robinson's Cairn

High Level Route

← detail →

Looking Stead

WASDALE HEAD ← direct route

1900

tarn

1800

WASDALE HEAD

1700

Black Sail Pass

1600

1500

1400

1300

1200

Ash Crag

River Liza

Sail Beck

1100

1000

Black Sail Y.H.

moraines

looking west

The main ridge, from Black Sail Pass to the summit, is a pleasant walk without difficulty, three stony rises being succeeded by splendid turf. A line of iron posts accompanies the ridge but the path, in many places, deviates to the left. The High Level route is a traverse across the fellside (aiming for Pillar Rock), not a way to the summit, although the two can be connected (see next page). This is a fine pedestrian way, highly recommended, rough but not difficult.

Originally the High Level Route had an awkward start. A new variation avoids the difficulty.

The path avoids the actual top of Looking Stead, but walkers should not. It is an excellent viewpoint for a survey, both of the High Level route and of Ennerdale.

There is a gate at the top of the pass but only a fanatical tourist would think of using it.

Sojourners at the hostel are fortunate in having Pillar on their doorstep, and can enjoy one of the best days of their young lives by climbing it.

Main ridge:
1: zigzag path
2: direct path
High Level route:
3: original start
4: new variation
Main ridge:
5: from Black Sail

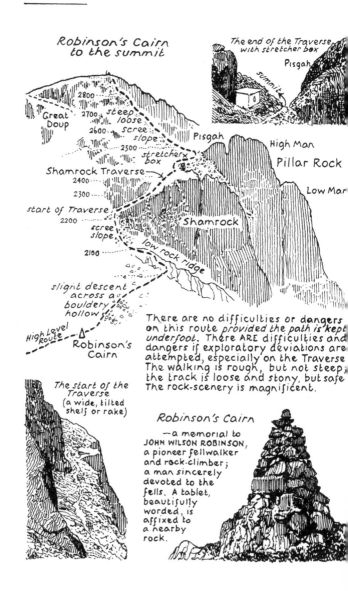

Robinson's Cairn
to the summit

The end of the Traverse
with stretcher box

Pisgah

summit

2800

Great
Doup

2700   steep
        loose
2600   scree
        slope   Pisgah

2500   High Man
        stretcher×
        box   Pillar Rock

Shamrock Traverse →
2400   Low Man

2300

start of Traverse
2200

scree
slope   Shamrock

2100   low rock ridge

slight descent
across a
bouldery
hollow

High Level
Route   △
        Robinson's
        Cairn

There are no difficulties or dangers
on this route *provided the path is kept
underfoot.* There ARE difficulties and
dangers if exploratory deviations are
attempted, especially on the Traverse
The walking is rough, but not steep,
the track is loose and stony, but safe
The rock-scenery is magnificent.

The start of the
Traverse
(a wide, tilted
shelf or rake)

Robinson's Cairn

—a memorial to
JOHN WILSON ROBINSON,
a pioneer fellwalker
and rock-climber;
a man sincerely
devoted to the
fells. A tablet,
beautifully
worded, is
affixed to
a nearby
rock.

ASCENT FROM ENNERDALE
(HIGH GILLERTHWAITE)

2500 feet of ascent
3¾ miles (A) : 2¾ miles (B)

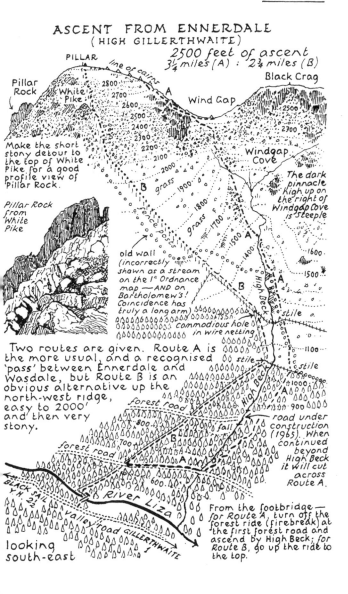

PILLAR

line of cairns

Pillar Rock

White Pike

Black Crag

Wind Gap

2800
2700
2600
2500
2400
2300
2200
2100
2000

2500
2300

Make the short stony detour to the top of White Pike for a good profile view of Pillar Rock.

Pillar Rock from White Pike

Windgap Cove

The dark pinnacle high up on the right of Windgap Cove is Steeple

grass
grass

1900
1800
1700
1600
1500
1400

High Beck

old wall (incorrectly shown as a stream on the 1" Ordnance map — AND on Bartholomew's! Coincidence has truly a long arm)

fence posts

commodious hole in wire netting

stile

Two routes are given. Route A is the more usual, and a recognised 'pass' between Ennerdale and Wasdale, but Route B is an obvious alternative up the north-west ridge, easy to 2000' and then very stony.

1100

stile
stile

1000

forest road

fall

800
700

600

forest road

900

road under construction (1965). When continued beyond High Beck it will cut across Route A.

River Liza

BLACK SAIL Y.H. 2¼

valley road GILLERTHWAITE

looking south-east

From the footbridge— for Route A, turn off the forest ride (firebreak) at the first forest road and ascend by High Beck; for Route B, go up the ride to the top.

ASCENT FROM ENNERDALE
(direct from THE MEMORIAL FOOTBRIDGE)

2250 feet of ascent
1¼ miles

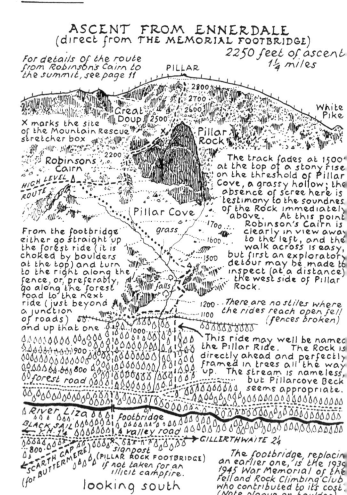

For details of the route from Robinson's Cairn to the summit, see page 11

PILLAR

White Pike

X marks the site of the Mountain Rescue stretcher box

Great Doup

Pillar Rock

2900
2700
2600
2500

2200

Robinsons Cairn

HIGH LEVEL ROUTE

Pillar Cove

grass

The track fades at 1500 at the top of a stony rise on the threshold of Pillar Cove, a grassy hollow; the absence of scree here is testimony to the soundness of the Rock immediately above. At this point Robinson's Cairn is clearly in view away to the left, and the walk across is easy, but first an exploratory detour may be made to inspect (at a distance) the west side of Pillar Rock.

From the footbridge either go straight up the forest ride (it is choked by boulders at the top) and turn to the right along the fence, or, preferably, go along the forest road to the next ride (just beyond a junction of roads) and up that one

1700
1600
1500

falls

1200
1100

There are no stiles where the rides reach open fell (fences broken)

This ride may well be named the Pillar Ride. The Rock is directly ahead and perfectly framed in trees all the way up. The stream is nameless, but Pillarcove Beck seems appropriate.

1000
900
800
forest road

River Liza
BLACK SAIL 1¼
800
SCARTH GAP
(for BUTTERMERE)

footbridge
valley road
signpost
(PILLAR ROCK FOOTBRIDGE)
if not taken for an illicit campfire.

GILLERTHWAITE 2¼

The footbridge, replacing an earlier one, is the 1939-1945 War Memorial of the Fell and Rock Climbing Club who contributed to its cost. (Note plaque on boulder).

looking south

A steep and rough, but romantic and adventurous climb in magnificent surroundings: the finest way up the mountain. Pillar Rock grips the attention throughout. Unfortunately the route is somewhat remote from tourist centres, but strong walkers can do it from Buttermere via Scarth Gap.

ASCENT FROM BUTTERMERE

Most walkers when planning to climb a mountain aim to avoid any downhill section between their starting-point and the summit, and if the intermediate descent is considerable the extra effort of regaining lost height may rule out the attempt altogether. A good example is Great Gable from Langdale, where the descent from Esk Hause to Sty Head is a loss of height of 700 feet and a double loss of this amount if returning to Langdale. Plus the 3000' of effective ascent this is too much for the average walker. Distance is of less consequence. The same applies to ascent of Pillar from Buttermere. This is a glorious walk, full of interest, but it cannot be done without first climbing the High Stile range (at Scarth Gap) and then descending into Ennerdale before setting foot on Pillar. If returning to Buttermere, Ennerdale and the High Stile range will have to be crossed again towards the end of an exhausting day. There is no sadder sight than a Buttermere-bound pedestrian crossing Scarth Gap on his hands and knees as the shadows of evening steal o'er the scene. The route is therefore recommended for strong walkers only.

The most thrilling line of ascent of Pillar is by way of the memorial footbridge, this being very conveniently situated for the Buttermere approach ('the bridge was, in fact, provided to give access to Pillar from this direction). A slanting route down to the footbridge leaves the Scarth Gap path some 150 yards on the Ennerdale side of the pass. The bifurcation is not clear, but the track goes off to the right above the plantation, becoming distinct and crossing the fences by three stiles. The climb from the bridge is described on the opposite page. A less arduous route of ascent is to keep to the Scarth Gap path into Ennerdale and climb out of the valley by Black Sail Pass to its top, where follow the ridge on the right — but this easier way had better be reserved for the return when energy is flagging.

To find the slanting path from Scarth Gap look for the rocky knoll, with tree (illustrated) and turn right on grass above it

Via the footbridge : 3550 feet of ascent : 5¼ miles
Via Black Sail Pass : 3250 feet of ascent : 6¼ miles

Pillar Rock, from the north

The Pillar Ride

THE SUMMIT

As in the case of many fells of rugged appearance, the summit is one of the smoothest places on Pillar, and one may perambulate within a 50-yard radius of the cairn without being aware of the declivities on all sides. There are stones, but grass predominates. The number of erections, including two wind-shelters and a survey column, testifies to the importance of the summit in the esteem of fellwalkers and map-makers.

DESCENTS :

To Wasdale Head : In fair weather or foul, there is one royal road down to Wasdale Head, and that is by the eastern ridge to join Black Sail Pass on its journey thereto. The views are superb, and the walking is so easy for the most part that they can be enjoyed while on the move. There should be no difficulty in following the path in mist — only in one cairned section is it indistinct — but the fence-posts are there in any event as a guide to the top of the Pass. Ten minutes can be saved by the short cut going down from the side of Looking Stead. The route into Mosedale via Wind Gap is much less satisfactory, and no quicker although shorter. Another way into Mosedale sometimes used is the obvious scree-gully opening off the ridge opposite the head of Great Doup, but why suffer the torture of a half-mile of loose stones when the ridge is so much easier and pleasanter ?

To Ennerdale : If bound for Black Sail Hostel, follow the eastern ridge to the pass, and there turn left on a clear path. If bound for Gillerthwaite or places west, follow the fence-posts northwest to White Pike and its ridge, which has a rough section of boulders below the Pike ; but in stormy weather prefer the route joining High Beck from Wind Gap.

To Buttermere : In clear weather, the direct route climbing up out of Ennerdale may be reversed ; at the forest road beyond the memorial footbridge walk up the valley for 120 yards, then taking a slanting path through the plantation on the left to Scarth Gap. In bad conditions, it is safer to go round by Black Sail Pass.

To any of the above destinations via Robinson's Cairn
Leave the summit at the north wind-shelter. Pillar Rock comes into view at once, and a rough loose track slithers down to the point where the first of its buttresses (Pisgah) rises from the fellside. Here turn right, by the stretcher-box (an excellent landmark) and along the Traverse to easy ground and the Cairn. On no account descend the hollow below the stretcher-box : this narrows to a dangerous funnel of stones and a sheer drop into a gully. (This is known as Walker's Gully, NOT because it is a gully for walkers, but because a man of this name fell to his death here).

PLAN OF THE SUMMIT

100 YARDS

WHITE PIKE · PILLAR ROCK · shelter · shelter · Great Doup · WIND GAP · 2900 · 2800 · BLACK SAIL PASS

Pillar Rock as seen from the north shelter

RIDGE ROUTES

To SCOAT FELL, 2760': 1¼ miles: WSW
Depression at 2480' (Wind Gap): 300 feet of ascent
A fine little journey in spectacular scenery.

After an indefinite start, a line of cairns leads down to Wind Gap, the last stage of the descent being steep and rough, but not difficult. Beyond the Gap a clear path goes up the facing slope into the boulders preceding the easy grassy promenade along the top above Black Crag. Then follows a slight loss of height before the final rise to Scoat Fell, the summit wall of which is joined in a chaotic pile of boulders.

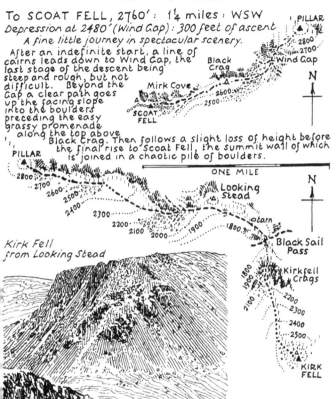

Kirk Fell from Looking Stead

To KIRK FELL, 2630': 2½ miles: ESE, then S
Depression at 1800' (Black Sail Pass): 850 feet of ascent
Excellent views, both near and far; a good walk

The Ennerdale fence (what is left of it) links the two tops, and the route never ventures far from it. The eastern ridge of Pillar offers a speedy descent, the path being clear except on one grassy section, which is, however, well cairned. At the Pass, the crags of Kirk Fell look ferocious and hostile, but a thin track goes off bravely to tackle them and can be relied upon to lead to the dull top of Kirk Fell after providing a minor excitement where a high rock step needs to be surmounted.

THE VIEW

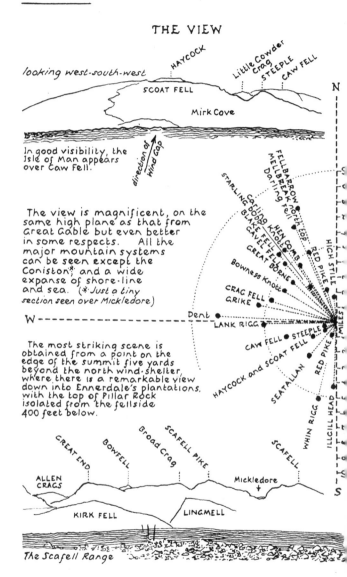

looking west-south-west

HAYCOCK

Little Cowder Crag · STEEPLE · CAW FELL

SCOAT FELL

Mirk Cove

N

In good visibility, the Isle of Man appears over Caw Fell.

direction of Wind Gap

FELLBARROW
MELLBREAK · Hen Cop
Darling Fell
STARLING DODD
CARLING KNOTT
BLAKE FELL
HEN COMB
GAVEL FELL
GREAT BORNE
HIGH STILE
RED PIKE

Bowness Knott

CRAG FELL
GRIKE

Dent

LANK RIGG

CAW FELL · STEEPLE
HAYCOCK and SCOAT FELL

The view is magnificent, on the same high plane as that from Great Gable but even better in some respects. All the major mountain systems can be seen except the Coniston*, and a wide expanse of shore-line and sea. (*Just a tiny section seen over Mickledore)

W - - - - - - - - - -

MILES

SEATALLAN

RED PIKE

WHIN RIGG

ILLGILL HEAD

The most striking scene is obtained from a point on the edge of the summit five yards beyond the north wind-shelter, where there is a remarkable view down into Ennerdale's plantations, with the top of Pillar Rock isolated from the fellside 400 feet below.

S

GREAT END
BOWFELL
Broad Crag
SCAFELL PIKE
SCAFELL

ALLEN CRAGS

Mickledore

KIRK FELL

LINGMELL

The Scafell Range

THE VIEW

Principal Fells

Lakes and Tarns

SSE: *Eel Tarn*
SSE: *Burnmoor Tarn*
WNW: *Ennerdale Water*
NNW: *Loweswater*

Innominate Tarn on Haystacks, ENE, is brought in the view by walking 10 yards from the column eastwards

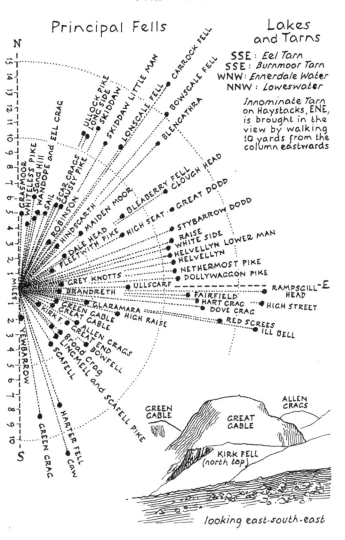

looking east-south-east

Place Fell

from Birks

Howtown •

▲ PLACE FELL

• Patterdale

MILES
0 1 2 3

Few fells are so well favoured as Place Fell for appraising neighbouring heights. It occupies an exceptionally good position in the curve of Ullswater, in the centre of a great bowl of hills; its summit commands a very beautiful and impressive panorama. On a first visit to Patterdale, Place Fell should be an early objective, for no other viewpoint gives such an appreciation of the design of this lovely corner of Lakeland.

NATURAL FEATURES

Place Fell rises steeply from the curve formed by the upper and middle reaches of Ullswater and its bulky mass dominates the head of the lake. Of only moderate elevation, and considerably overtopped by surrounding heights, nevertheless the fell more than holds its own even in such a goodly company: it has that distinctive blend of outline and rugged solidity characteristic of the true mountain. Many discoveries await those who explore: in particular the abrupt western flank, richly clothed with juniper and bracken and heather, and plunging down to the lake in a rough tumble of crag and scree, boulders and birches, is a paradise for the scrambler, while a more adventurous walker will find a keen enjoyment in tracing the many forgotten and overgrown paths across the fellside and in following the exciting and airy sheep-tracks that so skilfully contour the steep upper slopes below the hoary crest.

The eastern face, overlooking Boardale, is riven by deepcut gullies and is everywhere steep. Northward two ridges descend more gradually to the shores of Ullswater after passing over minor summits; from a lonely hollow between them issues the main stream on the fell, Scalehow Beck, which has good waterfalls. To the south, Boardale Hause is a well-known walkers' crossroads, and beyond this depression high ground continues to climb towards the principal watershed.

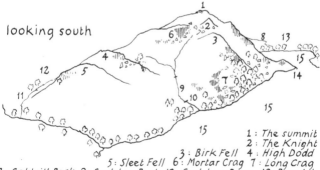

looking south

1 : The summit
2 : The Knight
3 : Birk Fell 4 : High Dodd
5 : Sleet Fell 6 : Mortar Crag 7 : Long Crag
8 : Goldrill Beck 9 : Scalehow Beck 10 : Scalehow Force 12 : Boardale
11 : Boardale Beck 13 : Patterdale 14 : Silver Point 15 : Ullswater

MAP

It is the author's opinion that the
lakeside path from Scalehow Beck,
near Sandwick, to Patterdale (in
that direction) is the most
beautiful and rewarding
walk in Lakeland.
  The junction of paths at
Silver Bay is indistinct
and easily missed.
The higher (east)
path branches
off left 70 yards
short of the beck
running into the bay.

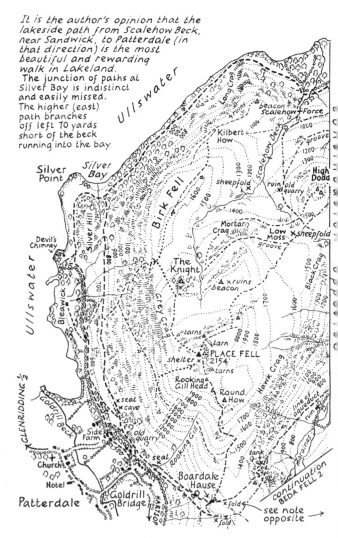

see note
opposite →

MAP

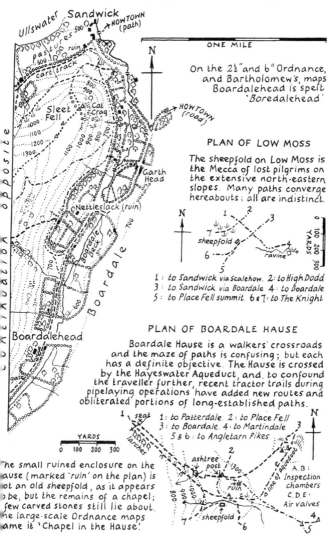

ONE MILE

On the 2½" and 6" Ordnance, and Bartholomew's maps Boardalehead is spelt 'Boredalehead'

PLAN OF LOW MOSS

The sheepfold on Low Moss is the Mecca of lost pilgrims on the extensive north-eastern slopes. Many paths converge hereabouts; all are indistinct.

1 : to Sandwick via Scalehow. 2: to High Dodd.
3 : to Sandwick via Boardale 4 : to Boardale
5 : to Place Fell summit. 6 & 7: to The Knight

PLAN OF BOARDALE HAUSE

Boardale Hause is a walkers' crossroads and the maze of paths is confusing; but each has a definite objective. The Hause is crossed by the Hayeswater Aqueduct, and, to confound the traveller further, recent tractor trails during pipelaying operations have added new routes and obliterated portions of long-established paths.

1: to Patterdale. 2: to Place Fell
3: to Boardale. 4: to Martindale
5 & 6: to Angletarn Pikes

A.B.: Inspection chambers
C.D.E.: Air valves

The small ruined enclosure on the Hause (marked 'ruin' on the plan) is not an old sheepfold, as it appears to be, but the remains of a chapel; a few carved stones still lie about. The large-scale Ordnance maps name it 'Chapel in the Hause'.

ASCENT FROM PATTERDALE
1700 feet of ascent : 1¼ miles

The face of Place Fell overlooking Patterdale is unremittingly and uncompromisingly steep, and the ascent is invariably made by way of the easier gradients of Boardale Hause, there being a continuous path on this route. (From the valley there appear to be paths going straight up the fell, but these are not paths at all: they are incipient streams and runnels). As an alternative, an old neglected track that branches from the higher path to Silver Bay is recommended: this slants leftwards to the skyline depression between Birk Fell and Grey Crag, the easy remainder of the climb then following without the help of a path. This old track is difficult to locate from above and it is better not used for descent as there is rough ground in the vicinity.

looking north-north-east

The diversion of the old track from the higher path to Silver Bay is not distinct: it occurs a full half-mile beyond the quarry at a point where there is a bluff of grey rock on the left above some larches. A flat boulder marks the junction, and a few ancient cairns along the route are a help. Botanists will find much of interest here.

Note also, 200 yards up the old track, a faint path turning away on the right: this climbs high across the face below Grey Crag, is lost on scree, but can be traced beyond, on the 1500' contour, all the way to the usual route via Boardale Hause — an exhilarating high-level walk. From this path the summit may be gained without difficulty after leaving Grey Crag behind and crossing a small ravine.

On the Boardale Hause route, take the upper path at the fork near the seat. Watch for the zigzag: if this is missed the walker naturally gravitates to the lower path. The prominent ashtree is on the upper path.

One cannot sojourn at Patterdale without looking at Place Fell and one cannot look long at Place Fell without duly setting forth to climb it. The time is very well spent.

ASCENT FROM SANDWICK
1700 feet of ascent : 2½ miles

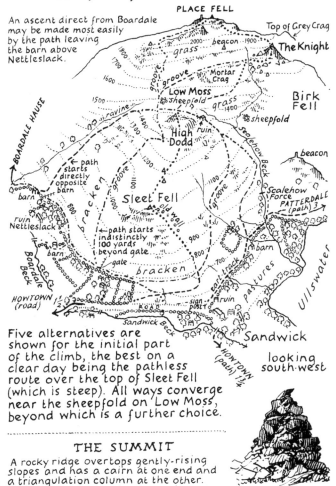

An ascent direct from Boardale may be made most easily by the path leaving the barn above Nettleslack.

PLACE FELL

Top of Grey Crag

The Knight

grass · beacon · 1900

2000

1800

1700

1600

1500

groove · Mortar Crag

Low Moss · sheepfold

grass · 1400

Birk Fell

sheepfold

1400

ravine

High Dodd · ruin

1300

1200

BOARDALE HAUSE

← path starts directly opposite barn

barn

groove

Sleet Fell · old wall

1100

groove

Scalehow Beck

beacon

Scalehow Force · PATTERDALE (path) 3

ruin Nettleslack

barn

← path starts indistinctly 100 yards beyond gate

900

gate

800

bracken

700

cart track

barn

pastures

Ullswater

Boardale Beck

HOWTOWN (road) ½ ½

sign-post

ruin

Sandwick Beck

HOWTOWN (path) 1¼

Sandwick

looking south-west

Five alternatives are shown for the initial part of the climb, the best on a clear day being the pathless route over the top of Sleet Fell (which is steep). All ways converge near the sheepfold on Low Moss, beyond which is a further choice.

THE SUMMIT
A rocky ridge overtops gently-rising slopes and has a cairn at one end and a triangulation column at the other. Many tarns adorn the top of the fell.
DESCENTS : Routes of descent are indicated in the illustration of the view; that to Boardale Hause is safest in bad weather.

THE VIEW

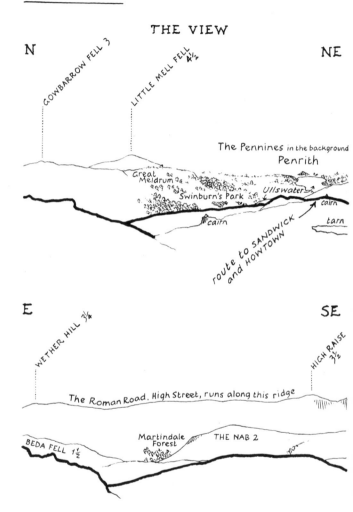

The thick line marks the visible boundaries
of Place Fell from the summit·cairn.
The figures following the names of fells
indicate distances in miles.

THE VIEW

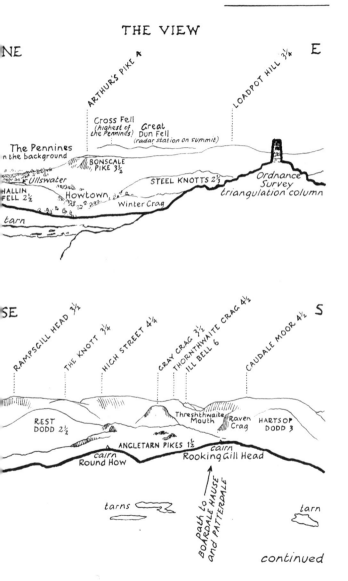

NE

ARTHUR'S PIKE ▲

Cross Fell
(highest of
the Pennines)

Great
Dun Fell
(radar station on summit)

LOADPOT HILL 3½

E

The Pennines
in the background

BONSCALE
PIKE 3½

Ullswater

HALLIN
FELL 2½

Howtown

STEEL KNOTTS 2⅔

Winter Crag

Ordnance
Survey
triangulation column

tarn

SE

RAMPSGILL HEAD 3½

THE KNOTT 3¾

HIGH STREET 4¼

GRAY CRAG 3½
THORNTHWAITE CRAG 4½
ILL BELL 6

CAUDALE MOOR 4½

S

REST
DODD 2½

Threshthwaite
Mouth

Raven
Crag

HARTSOP
DODD 3

ANGLETARN PIKES 1½

cairn
Round How

cairn
Rooking Gill Head

tarns

PATH TO BORDALE HAUSE AND PATTERDALE

tarn

continued

THE VIEW

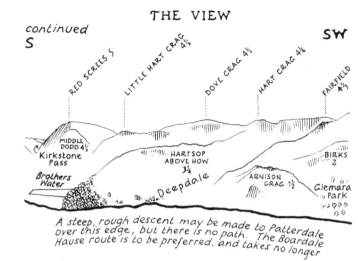

continued
S

SW

RED SCREES 5
LITTLE HART CRAG 4½
DOVE CRAG 4½
HART CRAG 4¼
FAIRFIELD 4⅓

MIDDLE DODD 4½
Kirkstone Pass
Brothers Water

HARTSOP ABOVE HOW 3¼

Deepdale

ARNISON CRAG 1½

BIRKS 2

Glemara Park

A steep, rough descent may be made to Patterdale
over this edge, but there is no path. The Boardale
Hause route is to be preferred, and takes no longer

W

NW

RAISE 2¾
STYBARROW DODD 4
GREAT DODD 4½
SKIDDAW 11¾

Sticks Pass

Green side
HART SIDE 3⅓
Brown Hills

CLOUGH HEAD 5½

SHEFFIELD PIKE 2⅔

Lead Mine

GLENRIDDING DODD 1½

Glencoyne

Glencoyne Wood

Glencoyne Park

Glenridding

Ullswater

Ullswater

Grey Crag is below this edge
(no descents here!)

THE VIEW

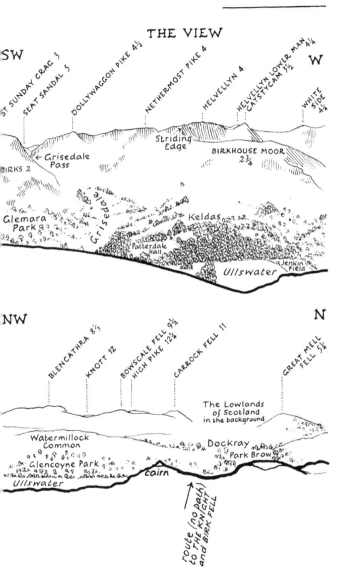

SW

ST SUNDAY CRAG 3
SEAT SANDAL 5
DOLLYWAGGON PIKE 4½
NETHERMOST PIKE 4
HELVELLYN 4
HELVELLYN LOWER MAN 4¼
CATSTYCAM 3½
WHITE SIDE 4½

W

Striding Edge

← Grisedale Pass

BIRKS 2

BIRKHOUSE MOOR 2¾

Glemara Park

Grisedale

Keldas

Patterdale Hall

Ullswater

Jenkin Field

NW

BLENCATHRA 8⅓
KNOTT 12
BOWSCALE FELL 9½
HIGH PIKE 12¼
CARROCK FELL 11
GREAT MELL FELL 5¼

N

The Lowlands of Scotland in the background

Watermillock Common

Dockray

Park Brow

Glencoyne Park

Ullswater

cairn

route (no path) to THE KNIGHT and BIRK FELL

Scafell

3162'

formerly Scawfell or Scaw Fell
(pronounced Scawfle)

from Cam Spout

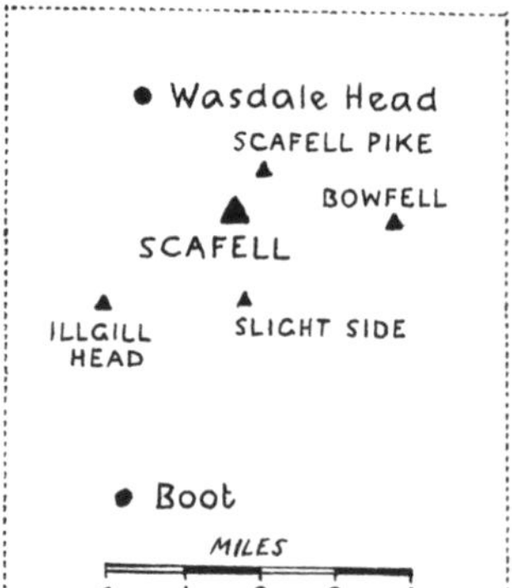

• Wasdale Head
SCAFELL PIKE ▲
▲ BOWFELL
▲
SCAFELL
▲ ILLGILL
HEAD
▲ SLIGHT SIDE

• Boot

MILES
0   1   2   3   4

NATURAL FEATURES

When men first named the mountains, the whole of the high mass south of Sty Head was known as Scaw Fell; later, as the work of the dalesfolk took them more and more onto the heights and closer identification became necessary, they applied the name to the mountain that seemed to them the greatest, the other summits in the range, to them individually inferior, being referred to collectively as the Pikes of Scaw Fell. Many folk today, even with the added knowledge that the main Pike is not only higher but actually the highest land in the country, share the old opinion that Scaw Fell (now Scafell) is the superior mountain of the group.

This respect is inspired not by the huge western flank going down to Wasdale nor by the broad southern slopes ending in the Eskdale foothills but rather by the towering rampart of shadowed crags facing north and east below the summit, the greatest display of natural grandeur in the district, a spectacle of massive strength and savage wildness but without beauty, an awesome and a humbling scene. A man may stand on the lofty ridge of Mickledore, or in the green hollow beneath the precipice amongst the littered debris and boulders fallen from it, and witness the sublime architecture of buttresses and pinnacles soaring into the sky, silhouetted against racing clouds or, often, tormented by writhing mists, and, as in a great cathedral, lose all his conceit. It does a man good to realise his own insignificance in the general scheme of things, and that is his experience here.

Fuller notes on the topography are contained in the Scafell Pike chapter

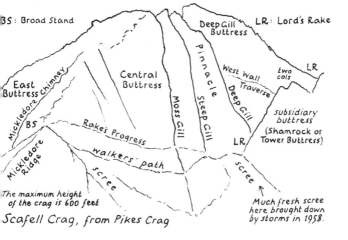

BS: Broad Stand   LR: Lord's Rake

The maximum height of the crag is 600 feet

Much fresh scree here brought down by storms in 1958.

Scafell Crag, from Pikes Crag

Scafell 3

Broad Stand

entrance

Broad Stand and Mickledore

The greatest single obstacle confronting ridge-walkers on the hills of Lakeland is the notorious Broad Stand, with which every traveller from Scafell Pike to Scafell comes face to face at the far end of the Mickledore traverse. Obstacles met on other ridges can be overcome or easily by-passed; not so Broad Stand. It is an infuriating place, making a man angry with himself for his inability to climb the thirty feet of rock that bar his way to the simple rising slope beyond. From a distance it looks nothing; close at hand it still looks not much to worry about; but with the first platform underfoot, while still not seeming impossible, the next awkward movement to the left plus an uneasy fear of worse hazards above and as yet unseen, influences sensible walkers to retreat from the scene and gain access to Scafell's top by using one or the other of the two orthodox pedestrian routes (via Lord's Rake or Foxes Tarn), each of which entails a long detour and, unfortunately, a considerable descent.

Nevertheless, Broad Stand has a long history and a lot of stories to its name, and it should at least be visited. Where the Mickledore ridge abuts against the broken crags of Scafell turn down the scree on the Eskdale side (east) and in no more than a dozen yards a deep vertical cleft, paved with stones, can be entered and passed through to a small platform. This cleft is a tight squeeze, well named as "Fat Man's Agony", and ladies, too, whose statistics are too vital, will have an uncomfortable time in it. The platform is shut in by smooth walls, the route of exit (for experts only) being up the scratched corner on the left. But for mere pedestrians the platform is the limit of their exploration and they should return through the cleft, resolving, as is customary, to do the climb next time. The author first made this resolve in 1930 and has repeated it a score of times since then; his continuing disappointment is amply compensated by the pleasure of going on living.

YOU HAVE BEEN WARNED!

Lord's Rake

Lord's Rake is a classic route, uncomfortable underfoot but magnificent all around. It is used on the ascent of Scafell from Wasdale Head via Brown Tongue and on the traverse of the main ridge. The Rake is unique, and one's fellwalking education is not complete until its peculiar delights and horrors have been experienced.

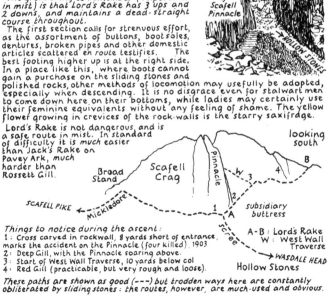

Strangers to Scafell may have some difficulty in locating the Rake, small-scale maps being unable to supply the details, but users of this book will have no such worries, of course.

The Rake starts (in ascent) as a steep, wide scree-gully or channel rising *not into* the mountain but obliquely across it and between the main crag and a subsidiary buttress, the top edge of which forms a parapet to the Rake. This first section is almost 100 yards in length, and ends at a perfect little col, so narrow that it can be straddled. A descent of 10 feet and a rise of 20 feet leads in 20 yards to another col, equally sweet, and the end of the Rake is now in sight 100 yards ahead and at the same elevation, although a steep descent to a stony amphitheatre is necessary before the exit can be reached. Here, now, is the open fell, and a rough track (left) leads to the top of Scafell.

The great thing to remember (important in mist) is that Lord's Rake has 3 ups and 2 downs, and maintains a dead-straight course throughout.

The first section calls for strenuous effort, as the assortment of buttons, boot-soles, dentures, broken pipes and other domestic articles scattered en route testifies. The best footing higher up is at the right side. In a place like this, where boots cannot gain a purchase on the sliding stones and polished rocks, other methods of locomotion may usefully be adopted, especially when descending. It is no disgrace even for stalwart men to come down here on their bottoms, while ladies may certainly use their feminine equivalents without any feeling of shame. The yellow flower growing in crevices of the rock-walls is the starry saxifrage.

Lord's Rake is not dangerous, and is a safe route in mist. In standard of difficulty it is *much easier* than Jack's Rake on Pavey Ark, much harder than Rossett Gill.

Things to notice during the ascent:
1 : Cross carved in rockwall, 8 yards short of entrance, marks the accident on the Pinnacle (four killed), 1903
2 : Deep Gill, with the Pinnacle soaring above.
3 : Start of West Wall Traverse, 10 yards below col
4 : Red Gill (practicable, but very rough and loose).

A-B : Lord's Rake
W : West Wall Traverse

These paths are shown as good (---) but trodden ways here are constantly obliterated by sliding stones : the routes, however, are much-used and obvious.

MAP

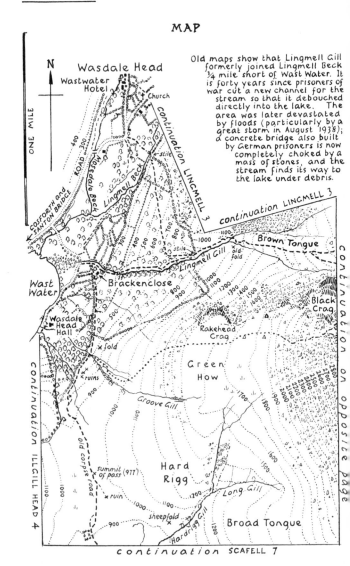

Old maps show that Lingmell Gill formerly joined Lingmell Beck ¼ mile short of Wast Water. It is forty years since prisoners of war cut a new channel for the stream so that it debouched directly into the lake. The area was later devastated by floods (particularly by a great storm in August 1938); a concrete bridge also built by German prisoners is now completely choked by a mass of stones, and the stream finds its way to the lake under debris.

ONE MILE

N

Wasdale Head

Wastwater Hotel

Church

continuation LINGMELL 3

COLFORTH and SANTON BRIDGE

ROAD

400

300

Wasdale Beck

Lingmell Beck

stile

continuation LINGMELL 3

700

600

500

1000

stile

1100

old fold

Brown Tongue

Lingmell Gill

Wast Water

Brackenclose

900

1200

1300

1400

1500

Black Crag

Wasdale Head Hall

fold

800

1000

Rakehead Crag

ruins

900

Green How

1900

2000

2100

2200

2300

continuation on opposite page

Groove Gill

1700

1800

1600

continuation ILLGILL HEAD 4

old corpse road

1000

summit of pass (977)

ruin

1000

sheepfold

900

Hard Rigg

1200

Long Gill

Hardrigg Gill

1200

Broad Tongue

1100

1500

1600

continuation SCAFELL 7

MAP

The inadequacy of maps to serve as a guide over rough and complicated ground, more especially where there are vertical elevations, is nowhere better illustrated than in the small area between Scafell and Scafell Pike. A lost and hapless wanderer standing on Mickledore ridge, trying to fit the tremendous scene around him into a half-inch space on his map, is deserving of every sympathy. So is the map-maker, furnished with many details and festooned with merging contours — and nowhere to put them; but this does not really excuse the rather nonchalant hachuring of crags on both the Ordnance Survey and Bartholomews maps, nor the omission of important paths. The map on this page is itself little better than useless. But never mind: there is a large-scale plan of this particular area on page 14 which, while not aspiring to portray the character of the terrain, should at least be informative enough to get the afore-mentioned hapless wanderer off Mickledore and on his way safely. It is a tribute to the place that it cannot be recorded properly on a map.

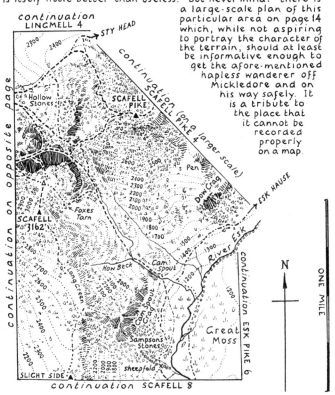

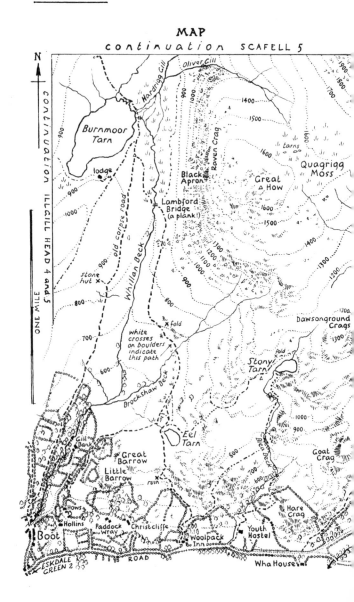

N

continuation ILLGILL HEAD 4 and 5

ONE MILE

Burnmoor Tarn

lodge

Hardriag Gill

Oliver Gill

900
1000
1400
1500
1600

Raven Crag

tarns

Quagrigg Moss

Black Apron

Great How

old corpse road

Lambford Bridge (a plank!)

1600
1500

Whillan Beck

1300
1200
1100
1000
900

stone hut ✕

1400
1300
1200

Dawsonground Crags

120a

800

800

✕ fold

white crosses on boulders indicate this path

fold

Stony Tarn

700

600

Brockshaw Beck

Eel Tarn

500

Great Barrow

Little Barrow

✕ ruin

1000
900

Black Beck

Goat Crag

Gill Bank

Hows

Hollins

Paddock wray

Christcliffe

Woolpack Inn

Hare Crag

Youth Hostel

Boot

ESKDALE GREEN 2

ROAD

Wha House

600

MAP

continuation SCAFELL 6

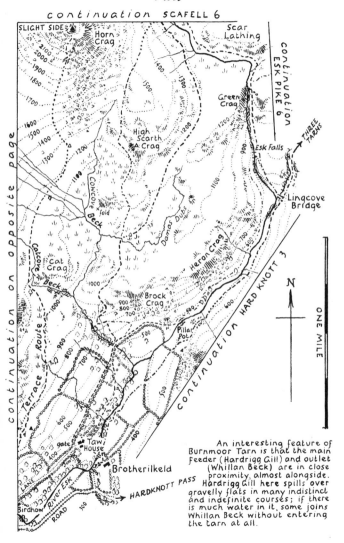

continuation ESK PIKE 6

continuation on opposite page

continuation HARD KNOTT 3

SLIGHT SIDE
Horn Crag
Scar Lathing
Green Crag
High Scarth Crag
THREE TARNS
Esk Falls
Concove Beck
Concove fold
Lingcove Bridge
Catcove Beck
Damas Dubs
Heron Crag
Cat Crag
Brock Crag
Pillar Pot
N
ONE MILE
Terrace Route
gate
Taw House
Brotherilkeld
HARDKNOTT PASS
Birdhow
LANE
River Esk
ROAD

An interesting feature of Burnmoor Tarn is that the main feeder (Hardrigg Gill) and outlet (Whillan Beck) are in close proximity, almost alongside. Hardrigg Gill here spills over gravelly flats in many indistinct and indefinite courses; if there is much water in it, some joins Whillan Beck without entering the tarn at all.

The head of Deep Gill
(the top of the descent to
the West Wall Traverse)
with the Pinnacle
(left-centre)
and the Oracle
(bottom right)

The West Wall Traverse

The massive crags of Scafell are split asunder by the tremendous
chasm of Deep Gill, which has two vertical pitches in its lower part
that put the through route out of bounds for walkers. The upper
half, however, although excessively stony, can be used by all and
sundry without difficulty, and is linked with Lord's Rake by a
simple path across a grassy shelf. This is the West Wall
Traverse. The rock scenery is awe-inspiring.

ASCENT: Go up the first section of Lord's
Rake. On the left, 10 yards short of the col,
a distinct path goes up to the grassy shelf,
along which it rises to enter Deep Gill, the
two pitches now being below. Steep scree
then follows to the open fell at the top of
the Gill. The exit used to be a desperate
scramble up a loose and earthy wall, but
clutching hands over the years have torn
down the cornice and escape is now easy,
especially on the left.

DESCENT: Go down into Deep Gill (easier
on the right), a descent not as bad as may
be thought from its appearance, but made
unpleasant by sliding stones. Watch for the
path turning left out of the Gill 80 yards down,
where the crag on this side eases off: this path
slants easily across a shelf into Lord's Rake. It
is vital that this path be taken; the Gill itself,
further down, drops vertically over chockstones
and is entirely impracticable for walkers.

SCAFELL
PIKE

col

The start of Lord's Ra
(in descen

ASCENT FROM WASDALE HEAD

via BROWN TONGUE: *3,000 feet of ascent : 3 miles*
via GREEN HOW:
2,950 feet : 3¾ miles
(from Wastwater Hotel)

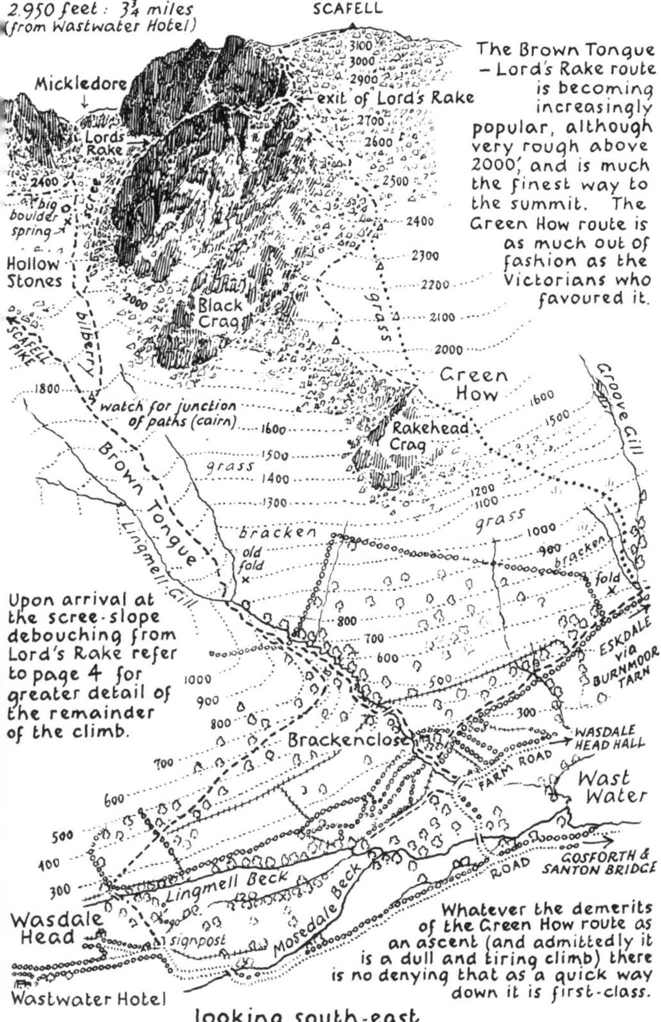

SCAFELL
3100
3000
2900
exit of Lord's Rake
2700
2600
2500
2400
2300
2200
2100
2000
Mickledore
Lords Rake
2400
big boulder
spring
scree
Hollow Stones
2000
Black Crag
SCAFELL PIKE
bilberry
grass
1800
watch for junction of paths (cairn)
1600
Green How
1600
1500
Groove Gill
Rakehead Crag
Brown Tongue
1500
grass
1400
1300
1200
1100
grass
Lingmell Gill
bracken
old fold
1000
900
bracken
fold
800
700
600
ESKDALE via BURNMOOR TARN
1000
900
500
300
800
Brackenclose
WASDALE HEAD HALL
700
FARM ROAD
Wast Water
600
500
400
GOSFORTH & SANTON BRIDGE
ROAD
300
Lingmell Beck
Mosedale Beck
Wasdale Head
signpost
Wastwater Hotel

The Brown Tongue – Lord's Rake route is becoming increasingly popular, although very rough above 2000', and is much the finest way to the summit. The Green How route is as much out of fashion as the Victorians who favoured it.

Upon arrival at the scree-slope debouching from Lord's Rake refer to page 4 for greater detail of the remainder of the climb.

Whatever the demerits of the Green How route as an ascent (and admittedly it is a dull and tiring climb) there is no denying that as a quick way down it is first-class.

looking south-east

ASCENT FROM ESKDALE
3100 feet of ascent : 6 miles from Boot

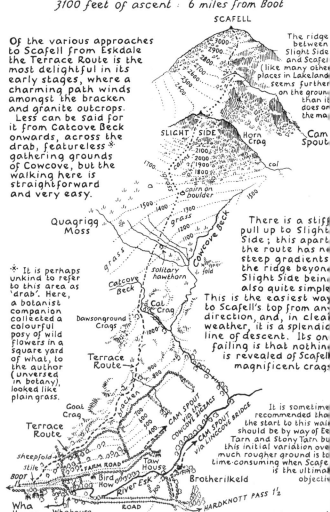

SCAFELL

Of the various approaches to Scafell from Eskdale the Terrace Route is the most delightful in its early stages, where a charming path winds amongst the bracken and granite outcrops.
Less can be said for it from Catcove Beck onwards, across the drab, featureless * gathering grounds of Cowcove, but the walking here is straightforward and very easy.

The ridge between Slight Side and Scafell (like many other places in Lakeland seems further on the ground than it does on the map

* It is perhaps unkind to refer to this area as 'drab'. Here, a botanist companion collected a colourful posy of wild flowers in a square yard of what, to the author (unversed in botany), looked like plain grass.

There is a stiff pull up to Slight Side; this apart the route has no steep gradients the ridge beyond Slight Side being also quite simple This is the easiest way to Scafell's top from any direction, and, in clear weather, it is a splendid line of descent. Its only failing is that nothing is revealed of Scafell magnificent crags

It is sometimes recommended that the start to this walk should be by way of Eel Tarn and Stony Tarn but this initial variation over much rougher ground is to time-consuming when Scafell is the ultimate objective

SLIGHT SIDE

Horn Crag

Cam Spout

col

cairn on boulder

cairns

grass

Cowcove Beck

Quagrigg Moss

grass

solitary hawthorn

fold

Catcove Beck

Cat Crag

Dawsonground Crags

Terrace Route

Goat Crag

Terrace Route

bracken

CAM SPOUT via the COWCOVE ZIGZAGS

CAM SPOUT via LINGCOVE BRIDGE

sheepfold
stile
BOOT 1¼

FARM ROAD

Taw House

Bird How

Brotherilkeld

River Esk

ROAD

HARDKNOTT PASS 1½

Wha House

Whahouse Bridge

looking north

ASCENT FROM ESKDALE
via CAM SPOUT
3050 feet of ascent : 7¼ miles from Boot

For a diagram and notes of the alternative routes to Cam Spout, see pages Scafell Pike 21 and 22.

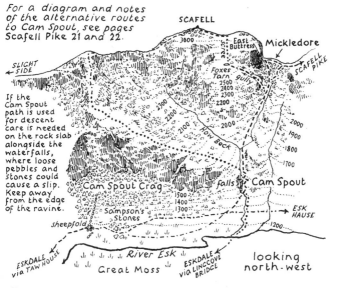

SCAFELL

3000

East Buttress

Mickledore

SCAFELL PIKE

SLIGHT SIDE

Foxes Tarn
2600
2500
2400
2300
2200

gully

2000
1900
1800
1700

2200
2200

How Beck

If the Cam Spout path is used for descent care is needed on the rock slab alongside the waterfalls, where loose pebbles and stones could cause a slip. Keep away from the edge of the ravine.

Cam Spout Crag

1500
1400
1300

Sampson's Stones

falls

Cam Spout

ESK HAUSE

1200

sheepfold

ESKDALE via TAW HOUSE

River Esk

Great Moss

ESKDALE via LINGCOVE BRIDGE

looking north-west

Take the scrambling route alongside the waterfalls, above which a good path goes up towards Mickledore, but before reaching the level of East Buttress and 100 yards below its nearest crags enter a stony gully going up squarely to the left; a small stream emerges from it. The gully, rough but not difficult, leads directly to Foxes Tarn (which is no more than a tiny pond with a large boulder in it), whence a long scree-slope is climbed to the saddle above, the top then being 250 easy yards distant. This is the quickest route to the summit from Cam Spout, and avoids the worst sections of the Mickledore screes.

Gluttons for punishment may, instead, continue up loose scree to the Mickledore ridge, descend the other side, and finish the climb by way of Lord's Rake, taking half an hour longer and making personal acquaintance with a few thousand more stones, but being rewarded by the finest scenery Scafell has to offer.

The pathless route along the curving ridge of Cam Spout Crag is very roundabout and the ridge itself is too broad to be exciting, although it narrows and becomes quite attractive near the end. The one advantage of this route, of importance to people with bunions, is that it is possible to walk on grass throughout, and in fact it is the only way to the main ridge of Scafell from Cam Spout that avoids scree entirely.

THE SUMMIT

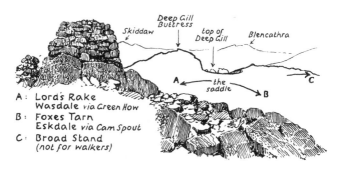

Deep Gill Buttress

Skiddaw

top of Deep Gill

Blencathra

A

the saddle

B

C

A: **Lord's Rake**
   Wasdale *via Green How*
B: **Foxes Tarn**
   Eskdale *via Cam Spout*
C: **Broad Stand**
   (not for walkers)

The face of Scafell Crag is the grandest sight in the district, and if only the highest point of the fell were situated on the top of Deep Gill Buttress, perched above the tremendous precipices of stone, it would be the best summit of all. As nature has arranged things, however, it lies back, away and remote from the excitement, the cairn being on a simple rise where there is little of interest at close quarters although the view southwards is enough to transfix the visitors attention for some minutes. On the south side of the cairn is a ruinous shelter, not now more serviceable as a protection against wind and rain than the cairn itself. The top is everywhere stony.

DESCENTS :

More than ordinary care is needed in choosing a route of descent. The western slope is stony, the eastern craggy, the northern precipitous. Except for Eskdale via Slight Side, recommended routes leave the saddle: turn left for Wasdale, right for Eskdale; go straight ahead for Deep Gill and the West Wall Traverse if Borrowdale is the objective *but only if the Traverse is already known; otherwise use Lords Rake.*
In mist, the Slight Side route may be tried, but if lost turn right down to Hardrigg Gill and the Burnmoor path. For other destinations aim for the saddle (big cairn) to which the path is clear but there is indistinct, and follow, cautiously, the fine-weather routes; see also map, page 14

SCAFELL

N

HALF A MILE

3100
3000
2900
2800
2700
2600
2500
2400

Long Green

CAM SPOUT

grass

SLIGHT SIDE

Horn Crag

RIDGE ROUTE

To SLIGHT SIDE, 2499' : 1¼ miles : S
Depression at 2400'
100 feet of ascent
   An easy walk, becoming pathless on grass.
In clear weather there is no difficulty. *In mist*, when the path fades, remember to keep the escarpment on the left hand throughout.

RIDGE ROUTE

To SCAFELL PIKE, 3210': 1¼ miles : compass useless.
750' of ascent via Lord's Rake, 900' via Foxes Tarn.
Loins should be girded up for an hour's hard labour.

There is no bigger trap for the unwary and uninformed walker than this. Scafell Pike is clearly in view but the intervening crags cannot be seen. The natural inclination will be to make a beeline for the Pike and to be deflected by the edge of the precipice down the easy slope to the right, encouraged by a good path that now appears. But this is the climbers' way to Broad Stand, which walkers cannot safely attempt. A desperate situation now arises. Just beyond the drop of Broad Stand, and tantalisingly near, is Mickledore Ridge, the easy connecting link between Scafell and the Pike. The choice is to risk a serious accident or toil all the way back and start again : not an easy decision for a walker already tired and pressed for time. The advice is to go back and start again.

From the grassy saddle (cairn) three routes are available :

1 : via LORD'S RAKE : This is the usual way, and it is arduous. Turn *left* down a slope that steepens and becomes all stones. The start of the Rake is further down the fellside than will generally be expected, and it should be identified exactly (see illustration, page 9). Avoid the gaping entrance to Red Gill midway. For details of the Rake, see page 4, where it is described in ascent — it will occur to the mentally alert that if there are 3 ups and 2 downs in the ascent there must be 3 downs and 2 ups in the descent. From the foot of the Rake continue ahead below the crags and scramble up to Mickledore Ridge, where turn left along a good path to the Pike.

2 : via FOXES TARN : This is easier, but involves a greater descent and re-ascent. Turn *right* down a steepening slope to the Tarn, then *left* by the issuing stream (rough gully) to join the stony path coming up from Cam Spout for Mickledore and the Pike (right).

3 : via THE WEST WALL TRAVERSE : This is something special. Consult the notes on page 9.

M : Mickledore Ridge
1 to 2 : Lord's Rake
3 : Deep Gill Buttress
4 : West Wall Traverse
5 : head of Deep Gill
6 : Mickledore Chimney
7 : Broad Stand
8 : Scafell Crag
9 : East Buttress

Map labels: LINGMELL COL — SCAFELL PIKE — 3100 — 3000 — N — 2900 — 2800 — HALF A MILE — Pikes Crag — Pulpit Rock — Hollow Stones — WASDALE — stony amphitheatre — subsidiary buttress 2 cols — 2500 — 2700 — GREEN HOW — head of narrow gully — watch for junction (keep right) — head of Red Gill — 3100 — SCAFELL ▲ — saddle — 3000 — 2900 — CAM SPOUT — Foxes Tarn (merely a small pool with a boulder in it)

Note that this map is on the scale of six inches to one mile. To assist clarity, areas of stones and boulders are omitted, but nobody should assume there aren't any : they occur all over the place.

THE VIEW

The bulky mass of Scafell Pike, north-east, obstructs the view of a considerable slice of Lakeland, but nevertheless Scafell's top is a most excellent viewpoint and, additionally, a place for reverie, especially when reached from the north, for here there is awareness that one has come at last to the outer edge of the mountains and that, beyond, lie only declining foothills to the sea. Vaguely, in the mind of a fellwalker long past his youth, there arises a feeling of sadness, as though at this point the mountains are behind, in the past, and ahead is a commonplace world, a future in which mountains have no part, his own future. Yet this vision of low hills and green valleys, of distant sands and wide expanses of sea, is very beautiful. From Morecambe Bay to Furness and across the Duddon Estuary and Black Combe to the sand dunes of Ravenglass, and along the glorious length of Eskdale, all is smiling and serene, often when the high mountains are frowning. The bright pastures of Eskdale, won from the rough fells, have a happy quality of seeming to be in sunlight even under cloud. The view in this direction, unmarred by any scars of industry, is superb.

The western fells, and the Bowfell and Coniston groups, all show to advantage. Look in particular for the little hidden valley of Miterdale, rarely seen but from this viewpoint, and no other, disclosed in its full length. On a clear day the Isle of Man may be seen above and to the left of Calder Hall atomic power station — which is too conspicuous — and the Solway Firth, backed by the Scottish hills, overtops Kirk Fell. Beyond Bowfell and Crinkle Crags the Pennines are visible. Most visitors look for Helvellyn in every view, but from Scafell's summit it is exactly covered by the south peak of Scafell Pike across Mickledore.

THE VIEW

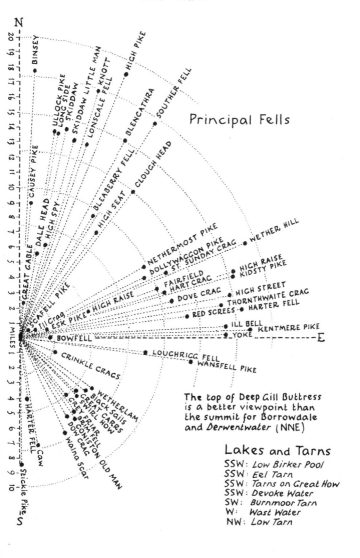

Principal Fells

The top of Deep Gill Buttress
is a better viewpoint than
the summit for Borrowdale
and *Derwentwater* (NNE)

Lakes and Tarns
SSW: *Low Birker Pool*
SSW: *Eel Tarn*
SSW: *Tarns on Great How*
SSW: *Devoke Water*
SW: *Burnmoor Tarn*
W: *Wast Water*
NW: *Low Tarn*

Scafell Pike

3210'

the highest mountain in England

formerly 'The Pikes' or 'The Pikes of Scawfell';
'Scafell Pikes' on Ordnance Survey maps.

from Great Moss,
Upper Eskdale

Scafell Pike

Ill Crag

from the gorge
of the Esk

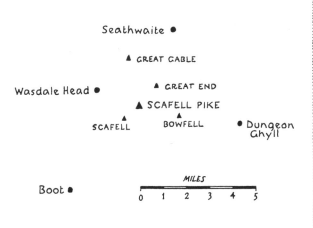

Seathwaite ●

▲ GREAT GABLE

Wasdale Head ●   ▲ GREAT END

▲ SCAFELL PIKE

▲ SCAFELL   ▲ BOWFELL   ● Dungeon
                                    Ghyll

Boot ●

MILES

0   1   2   3   4   5

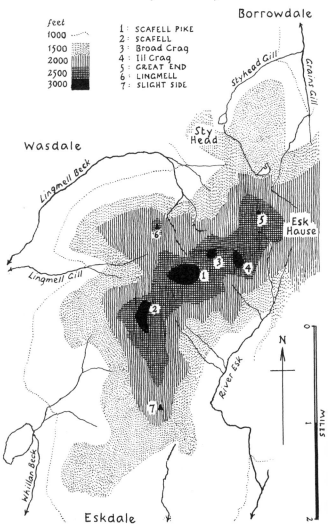

The Scafell Range

feet	
1000	(dotted)
1500	
2000	
2500	
3000	

1 : SCAFELL PIKE
2 : SCAFELL
3 : Broad Crag
4 : Ill Crag
5 : GREAT END
6 : LINGMELL
7 : SLIGHT SIDE

Scafell Pike's grandest crag:
Dow Crag

Known to climbers as Esk Buttress, this 400-foot near-vertical crag rises from the fellside low down on the mountain's east flank, overlooking the River Esk.

Scafell Pike's best-known crag:
Pulpit Rock

This fine pinnacle (seen here from Mickledore) is the best feature of Pikes Crag, above Hollow Stones. Its top (easily reached from the summit-to-Mickledore path) is the best of all viewpoints for Scafell Crag.

NATURAL FEATURES

The difference between a hill and a mountain depends on *appearance*, not on *altitude* (whatever learned authorities may say to the contrary) and is thus arbitrary and a matter of personal opinion. Grass predominates on a hill, rock on a mountain. A hill is smooth, a mountain rough. In the case of Scafell Pike, opinions must agree that here is a mountain without doubt, and a mountain that is, moreover, every inch a mountain. Roughness and ruggedness are the necessary attributes, and the Pike has these in greater measure than other high ground in the country —— which is just as it should be, for there is no higher ground than this.

Strictly, the name 'Scafell Pike' should be in the plural, there being three principal summits above 3000 feet, the two lesser having the distinguishing titles of Broad Crag and Ill Crag. The main Pike is, however, pre-eminent, towering over the others seemingly to a greater extent than the mere 160 feet or so by which it has superiority in altitude, and in general being a bulkier mass altogether.

The three summits rise from the main spine of an elevated ridge which keeps above 2800 feet to its abrupt termination in the cliffs of Great End, facing north to Borrowdale; lower spurs then run down to that valley. In the opposite direction, southwest, across the deep gulf of Mickledore, is the tremendous rock-wall of the neighbouring and separate mountain of Scafell, which also exceeds 3000 feet: this is the parent mountain in the one sense that its name has been passed on to the Pikes. Scafell's summit-ridge runs south and broadens into foothills, descending ultimately to mid-Eskdale.

continued

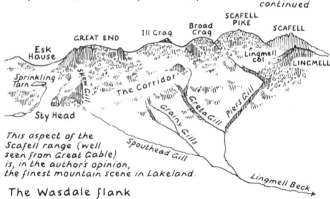

SCAFELL PIKE
Broad Crag
Ill Crag
GREAT END
SCAFELL
Esk Hause
Lingmell col
LINGMELL
Sprinkling Tarn
Skew Gill
The Corridor
Greta Gill
Piers Gill
Sty Head
Grainy Gills
Spouthead Gill
Lingmell Beck

This aspect of the Scafell range (well seen from Great Gable) is, in the author's opinion, the finest mountain scene in Lakeland.

The Wasdale flank

NATURAL FEATURES

The flanks of the range are bounded on the west by Wasdale, and by the upper reaches of Eskdale, east. All the waters from the Pikes (and from Scafell) flow into one or other of these two valleys, ultimately to merge in the Ravenglass estuary. Thus it will be seen that Scafell Pike, despite a commanding presence, has not the same importance, geographically, as many other fells in the district. It does not stand at the head of any valley, but between valleys: it is not the hub of a wheel from which watercourses radiate; it is one of the spokes. It is inferior, in this respect, to Great Gable or Bowfell nearby, or even its own Great End.

Another interesting feature of Scafell Pike is that although it towers so mightily above Wasdale it can claim no footing in that valley, its territory tapering quickly to Brown Tongue, at the base of which it is nipped off by the widening lower slopes of Lingmell and Scafell.

Tarns are noticeably absent on the arid, stony surface of the mountain, but there is one sheet of water below the summit to the south, Broadcrag Tarn, which is small and unattractive, but, at 2725 feet, can at least boast the highest standing water in Lakeland.

Crags are in evidence on all sides, and big areas of the upper slopes lie devastated by a covering of piled-up boulders, a result not of disintegration but of the volcanic upheavals that laid waste to the mountain during its formation. The landscape is harsh, even savage, and has attracted to itself nothing of romance or historical legend. There is no sentiment about Scafell Pike.

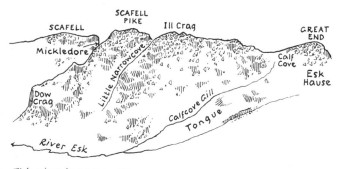

This view is as seen from the south ridge of Esk Pike

The Eskdale flank

MAP

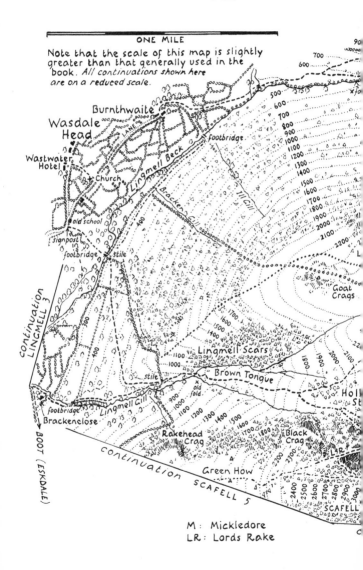

ONE MILE

Note that the scale of this map is slightly greater than that generally used in the book. All continuations shown here are on a reduced scale.

M : Mickledore
LR : Lords Rake

MAP

A : to BORROWDALE
B : to GREAT LANGDALE

C : to ESKDALE
(via CAM SPOUT)

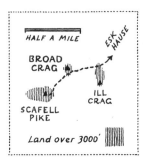

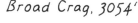
Broad Crag, 3054'

Broad Crag is the second of the Scafell Pikes, and a worthy mountain in itself — but it has little fame, is not commonly regarded as a separate fell, and its summit is rarely visited. This latter circumstance appears strange, because the blazed highway between Esk Hause and the main Pike not only climbs over the shoulder of Broad Crag but actually passes within a hundred yards of its summit, which is not greatly elevated above the path. Yet not one person in a thousand passing along here (and thousands do!) turns aside to visit the cairn. The reason for this neglect is more obvious when on the site than it is from a mere study of the map, for the whole of the top is littered deep with piled boulders across which it is quite impossible to walk with any semblance of dignity, the detour involving a desperate and inelegant scramble and the risk of breaking a leg at every stride. Most walkers using the path encounter enough trouble underfoot without seeking more in the virgin jungle of tumbled rock all around. Broad Crag is, in fact, the roughest summit in Lakeland.

The eastern slope descends into Little Narrowcove, and is of small consequence, but the western flank is imposing. On this side the top breaks away in a semi-circle of crags, below which is a shelf traversed by the Corridor Route and bounded lower down a steepening declivity by the great gash of Piers Gill.

Only the proximity of the main Scafell Pike, overtopping the scene, robs Broad Crag of its rightful place as one of the finest of fells.

Broad Crag, and Broad Crag col (right)
from the Corridor Route

Ill Crag, 3040'

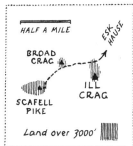

HALF A MILE

ESK HAUSE

BROAD CRAG

ILL CRAG

SCAFELL PIKE

Land over 3000'

Ill Crag is the third of the Scafell Pikes, and the most shapely, appearing as a graceful peak when viewed from upper Eskdale, which it dominates. Like Broad Crag, the summit lies off the path from Esk Hause to the main Pike but is more distant, although in this case too the shoulder of the fell is crossed at a height exceeding 3000', so that the summit is raised but little above it. The detour to the top is simple, only the final short rise being really rougher than the boulder-crossings on the path itself. Ill Crag is prominently seen from the vicinity of Esk Hause, and many wishful (and subsequently disappointed) walkers hereabouts, engaged on their first ascent of Scafell Pike will wrongly assume it to be their objective.

The western slope goes down uneventfully between Broad Crag and Great End to the Corridor Route, and the glory of the fell is its excessively steep and rough fall directly from the cairn eastwards into the wilderness of upper Eskdale: a chaotic and desolate scene set at a precipitous gradient, a frozen avalanche of crags and stones, much of it unexplored and uncharted, wild in the extreme, and offering a safe refuge for escaped convicts or an ideal depository for murdered corpses. Someday, when the regular paths become overcrowded, it may be feasible to track out an exciting and alternative route of ascent for scramblers here, but the author prefers to leave the job to someone with more energy and a lesser love of life.

Ill Crag, from the path above Esk Hause

Pikes Crag
Pulpit Rock
Mickledore Buttress
Mickledore
Scafell Crag

from Hollow Stones

Once in a while every keen fellwalker should have a *pre-arranged* night out amongst the mountains. Time drags and the hours of darkness can be bitterly cold, but to be on the tops at dawn is a wonderful experience and much more than recompense for the temporary discomfort.

Hollow Stones is an excellent place for a bivouac, with a wide choice of overhanging boulders for shelter, many of which have been walled-up and made draught-proof by previous occupants. Watch the rising sun flush Scafell Crag and change a black silhouette into a rosy-pink castle! (This doesn't always happen. Sometimes it never stops raining).

Not many readers, not even those who are frequent visitors to Scafell Pike could give a caption to this picture. It is, in fact, a scene in the unfrequente hollow of Little Narrowcove, looking up towards the summit of the Pike (th top cairn is out of sight). The crags, unsuspected on the usual routes, are a great surprise. Little Narrowcove (reached from Broad Crag col) is a grassy basin sheltered or encircled by cliffs: a good site for a mountain camp.

ASCENTS

The ascent of Scafell Pike is the toughest proposition the 'collector' of summits is called upon to attempt, and it is the one above all others that, as a patriot, he cannot omit. The difficulties are due more to roughness of the ground than to altitude, and to the remoteness of the summit from frequented valleys. From all bases except Wasdale Head the climb is long and arduous, and progress is slow: this is a full-day expedition, and the appropriate preparations should be made. Paths are good, but only in the sense that they are distinct; they are abominably stony, even bouldery — which is no great impediment when ascending but mitigates against quick descent. Ample time should be allowed for getting off the mountain.

In winter especially, when conditions can be Arctic, it is important to select a fine clear day, to start early, and keep moving; reserve three hours of daylight for the return journey. If under deep snow the mountain is better left alone altogether, for progress would then be laborious, and even dangerous across the concealed boulders, with a greater chance of death from exposure than of early rescue if an accident were to occur.

Scafell Pike may be ascended most easily from Wasdale Head, less conveniently from Borrowdale or Great Langdale or Eskdale. But all routes are alike in grandeur of scenery.

from WASDALE HEAD :
The usual route from Wasdale Head, via Brown Tongue, is the shortest way to the top from any inhabited place but also the dullest unless the opportunity is taken to visit Mickledore by a deviation from the trodden path, which may then be used throughout for descent. But consider the Corridor Route or Piers Gill to add variety to the walk.
*3 hours up,
2 down.*

from BORROWDALE :
The ascent from Borrowdale is pre-eminent, because not only is the scenery excellent throughout but there is the advantage of two interesting and well-contrasted routes, so that one may be used in ascent and the alternative in descent, the whole round, in settled weather, being perhaps the finest mountain-walk in the district. *From Seathwaite —
3½ hours up, 2½ down*

Since this book is intended to cater for all classes and conditions of walkers, it must be added that sufferers from bad feet must expect an orgy of torture on any of these ascents.

from GREAT LANGDALE :
This popular ascent suffers from the disadvantage that the route must be used both up and down, and the same ground thus trodden twice, by walkers based in the valley (this means Rossett Gill twice in one day!). Otherwise, this is a splendid expedition. *From Dungeon Ghyll — 4 hours up, 3 down.*

from ESKDALE :
This is the best line of approach to the mountain: from the south its grandest and most rugged aspect is seen. Variations of route may be adopted, but time is a great enemy: the walk is lengthy (a feature most noticed when returning). *From Boot — 4½ hours up, 3½ down.*

ASCENT FROM WASDALE HEAD
via BROWN TONGUE

3,000 feet of ascent
3½ miles
(from Wastwater Hotel)

SCAFELL PIKE

Dropping Crag

LINGMELL

Scafell Crag

Lingmell col

3100
3000

Pikes Crag

Mickledore

Corridor Route to STY HEAD

2600
2500

Pulpit Rock

Climbers' traverse

2400

grass line of cairns

2300
2200
2100
2000
1900

big boulder & spring

Hollow Stones

The tourist route goes round by Lingmell col and is a tiring and uninteresting grind, designed to preserve its users from fears and falterings. The path is good, well-cairned, and practicable in mist.

shelter amongst boulders

route to SCAFELL via LORD'S RAKE

Black Crag

If bound for Mickledore, look for the deviation on Brown Tongue (cairn on right) when almost at the level of Black Crag.

More enterprising walkers will deviate from the track up Brown Tongue into Hollow Stones and reach the summit by way of Mickledore, a journey as magnificent as the other is dull, although calling for rather more effort: the surround of crags is tremendously impressive, with Scafell Crag impending sensationally overhead. The ridge of Mickledore, gained by a steep scree gully, is the best place in Lakeland for viewing the vertical from the comfort and safety of the horizontal.
Either way, the last half-mile lies across stones.

bilberry

old path

1800
1700
1600
1500
1400
1300
1200
1100
1000
900

old fold

x old sheepfold

stile

Lingmell Gill

800
700
600
500

1000
900
800
700
600
500
400

bracken

footbridge

old fold xx
stiles
footbridge
old school
signpost

300

Brackenclose

WASDALE HEAD HALL

Lingmell Beck

LANE

Church

Mosedale Beck

Wast Water

Wastwater Hotel

ROAD

COSSFORTH & SANTON BRIDGE

Wasdale Head

looking east

ASCENT FROM WASDALE HEAD
via PIERS GILL

3,000 feet of ascent
3¾ miles
(from Wastwater Hotel)

SCAFELL PIKE

Broad Crag col

Broad Crag

Dropping Crag

LINGMELL

WASDALE

Lingmell col

3100
2800
2700
2600
2500
2400

At point B, either take the usual path via Lingmell col, or (a good alternative) follow the stream up to Broad Crag col, there joining the path from Esk Hause

STY HEAD (CORRIDOR ROUTE)

old wall

B

tarns

grass

scree

Middleboot Knotts

Criscliffe Knotts

2000

scree

Stand Crag

ravines

C

1600

Greta Gill

Piers Gill

1500
1400
1300
1200

grass

A

NOTE WELL THAT THERE IS NO THROUGH WAY ON THE WEST SIDE (true left) OF PIERS GILL, PROGRESS BEING BARRED BY CRAGS. NOR CAN THE GILL BE CROSSED BETWEEN POINTS A AND B. THE BED OF THE GILL IS ALSO IMPASSABLE.

1300
1400

grass

STY HEAD

Spouthead Gill

cairn on boulder

stream-bed

wide stone

1200
1100
1000

a beautiful watersmeet

pools and cascades

900

looking south

STY HEAD (direct route)

300

700

Use the Sty Head Valley Route (see Great End 7) and, after crossing at the watersmeet, take advantage of the zig-zags for 250 yards, where a cairn on a boulder indicates the start of an indistinct grassy trod along the east bank. A little doubt is likely to arise at point C, where a steepish wall of broken crag has to be negotiated alongside a conspicuous tongue of fresh scree, but there is easy scrambling only and no real difficulty in finding a way up. The edge of the great ravine may be, and should be, visited at opportune places for the striking views into its depths, but extreme care is necessary, as the sheer walls are badly eroded and dangerously loose.

The tremendous north face of Lingmell, gashed by the great ravine of Piers Gill, is enough justification for essaying this fine and rather adventurous route. The way is pathless alongside the gill; clear weather is advisable for ascent and essential for descent by this route.

moraines
footbridge

Lingmell Beck

500

600

Burnthwaite

WASTWATER HOTEL ½

Wasdale Head

ASCENT FROM BORROWDALE
via STY HEAD
3,000 feet of ascent
6 miles from Seatoller

Sty Head

Having duly arrived at Styhead Tarn (so proving the reliability of the diagram thus far) refer now (with confidence) to the foot of the next page for the continuation of the route.

Styhead Tarn

1600

1500

boulder

Patterson's Fold *(sheepfold)*

By keeping to the left of the many variations, a section of the original grooved and paved path will be found, and how superior it is to the modern 'short-cuts'!

1400

1300

Don't panic if unable to ford the stream here (normally easy); keep on along the west bank

The footbridge was originally sited 150 yards downstream, where the buttresses of the former bridge can still be seen.

cascades

ESK HAUSE

1100

1200

700

600

Taylorgill Force

The steep fell here is BASE BROWN

Stockley Bridge

Styhead Gill

Old folds

800

GREAT GABLE via GREEN GABLE

River Derwent

The crag high on the left is Hind Crag

gates

Seathwaite Slabs

Sourmilk Gill

Seathwaite

LANE

sheepfold

disused plumbago mines

one of the friendliest of farms. No need to fear the dogs or other animals here: visitors merely bore them.

The Borrowdale Yews ('the fraternal four')

Taylorgill Force

The lane to the footbridge here passes under the arch of the farm buildings.

ROAD

It is remarkable that the splendid variation route passing up through the gorge of Taylorgill Force has never found popular favour and is ignored by map-makers although it has been used by discerning walkers for many decades. This, compared with the usual Stockley Bridge path, is often rather wet in the lower intakes, a small disadvantage to set against its merits of quietness, quickness, sustained interest and waterfall and ravine scenery of high quality. A certain amount of delectable clambering on rocky sections of the path is likely to prohibit its use generally by all and sundry (including the many Sunday afternoon picnic parties), which is a good thing for the genuine fellwalker.

Seathwaite Bridge

gate

500

Few readers will need to refer to this page, as the walk to Sty Head is amongst the best-known in the district, this being evidenced by the severe wear and tear of the path.

River Derwent

ROAD

Seatoller

ROSTHWAITE 1·4

bus terminus

HONISTER PASS

looking south-south-west

ASCENT FROM BORROWDALE
via STY HEAD

continued

looking south

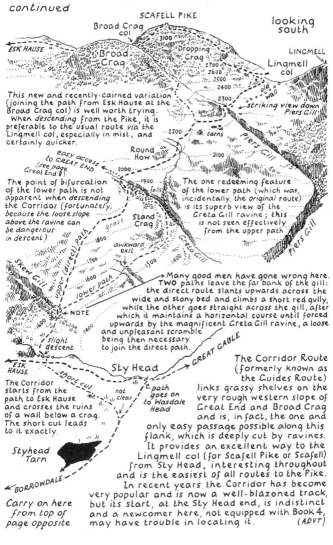

SCAFELL PIKE

Broad Crag col

Broad Crag

Dropping Crag

3100

2700
2600
2500
2400

2300

LINGMELL

Lingmell col

Lingmell

ESK HAUSE

old wall

striking view down Piers Gill

2200 tarns

Piers Gill

2100

Round How

2000

easy access to GREAT END (see page Great End 8)

1900 falls

Stand Crag

grass

awkward exit

1800

1700

1600

Skew Gill

upper (direct) path

lower path

NOTE

slight descent

Greta Gill

1500

1400

Piers Gill

This new and recently-cairned variation (joining the path from Esk Hause at the Broad Crag col) is well worth trying.

When *descending* from the Pike, it is preferable to the usual route *via* the Lingmell col, especially in mist, and certainly quicker.

The point of bifurcation of the lower path is not apparent when *descending* the Corridor (fortunately, because the loose slope above the ravine can be dangerous in descent.)

The one redeeming feature of the lower path (which was, incidentally, the *original* route) is its superb view of the Greta Gill ravine; this is not seen effectively from the upper path

Many good men have gone wrong here. **TWO** paths leave the far bank of the gill: the direct route slants upwards across the wide and stony bed and climbs a short red gully, while the other goes straight across the gill, after which it maintains a horizontal course until forced upwards by the magnificent Greta Gill ravine, a loose and unpleasant scramble being then necessary to join the direct path.

GREAT GABLE

ESK HAUSE

short cut

Sty Head

not clear

path goes on to Wasdale Head

The Corridor starts from the path to Esk Hause and crosses the ruins of a wall below a crag. The short cut leads to it exactly.

Styhead Tarn

BORROWDALE

Carry on here from top of page opposite

The Corridor Route (formerly known as the Guides Route) links grassy shelves on the very rough western slope of Great End and Broad Crag and is, in fact, the one and only easy passage possible along this flank, which is deeply cut by ravines. It provides an excellent way to the Lingmell col (for Scafell Pike or Scafell) from Sty Head, interesting throughout and is the easiest of all routes to the Pike.
In recent years the Corridor has become very popular and is now a well-blazoned track, but its start, at the Sty Head end, is indistinct and a newcomer here, not equipped with Book 4, may have trouble in locating it.   (ADVT)

ASCENT FROM BORROWDALE
via ESK HAUSE
3,200 feet of ascent : 5½ miles from Seatoller

A : A fairly new path cuts off the corner by the wall-shelter and is now in common use

B : Path continues behind Great End to Scafell Pike

The summit here is ALLEN CRAGS

D : Central Gully
C : South-east Gully

There is a lengthy dissertation concerning Esk Hause on pages Esk Pike 3 and 4, but not time enough to stop and read it when actually en route for Scafell Pike.

GLARAMARA is the long fell on the left of the valley

Note the strange rocky recess with waterfall on the east bank. An easier path crosses to the west bank just here

The fell bounding the valley on the right is SEATHWAITE FELL

The towering precipice of Great End increasingly dominates this section of the walk and, by the time Ruddy Gill (named from its red subsoil) is reached, assumes awe-inspiring proportions.

Cliff high on the left is Hind Crag

Great Gable comes into view at this point, but the gem of the scene hereabouts is the glorious vista of Derwentwater and Skiddaw, looking back over the line of approach.

Conspicuous waterfall (Taylorgill Force)

The fell on the right is BASE BROWN

Is it Grain Gill or Grains Gill? The signpost at Stockley Bridge omits the 's' (it also puts a 'w' in Scafell) but Grains is thought to be correct. At any rate, the floor of the valley here is named Grains, according to Ordnance maps.

The Borrowdale Yews (Wordsworth's 'fraternal four')

This diagram continues on the opposite page

looking south

ROSTHWAITE 1¼

HONISTER PASS

ASCENT FROM BORROWDALE
via ESK HAUSE

continued

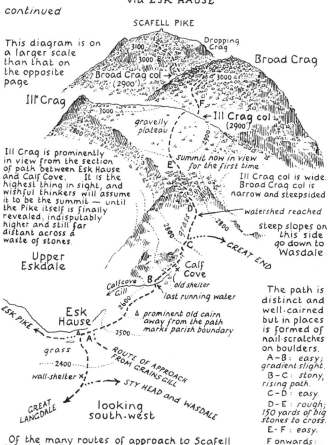

SCAFELL PIKE

This diagram is on a larger scale than that on the opposite page.

Dropping Crag

Broad Crag

3100
3000

Broad Crag col (2900')

Ill Crag

3000

2800

gravelly plateau

F

Ill Crag col (2900')

2900

summit now in view for the first time

E

Ill Crag is prominently in view from the section of path between Esk Hause and Calf Cove. It is the highest thing in sight, and wishful thinkers will assume it to be the summit — until the Pike itself is finally revealed, indisputably higher and still far distant across a waste of stones.

Upper Eskdale

Ill Crag col is wide. Broad Crag col is narrow and steepsided

watershed reached

2800

steep slopes on this side go down to Wasdale

D

2800

grass

C

GREAT END

Calf Cove

old shelter

B

last running water

Calfcove Gill

2600

△ *prominent old cairn away from the path marks parish boundary*

Esk Hause

A

2500

The path is distinct and well-cairned but in places is formed of nail-scratches on boulders.

A–B: easy; gradient slight.

B–C: stony, rising path.

C–D: easy.

D–E: rough; 150 yards of big stones to cross.

E–F: easy.

F onwards: excessively rough — inescapable boulders, stones and scree.

ESK PIKE

grass

2400

wall-shelter X

GREAT LANGDALE

ROUTE OF APPROACH FROM GRAINS GILL

STY HEAD and WASDALE

looking south-west

Of the many routes of approach to Scafell Pike, this, from Borrowdale *via* Esk Hause, is the finest. The transition from the quiet beauty of the valley pastures and woods to the rugged wildness of the mountain-top is complete, but comes gradually as height is gained and after passing through varied scenery, both nearby and distant, that sustains interest throughout the long march.

ASCENT FROM GREAT LANGDALE
3,400 feet of ascent : 5½ miles (from Dungeon Ghyll, Old Hotel

From Esk Hause onwards the route coincides with that from Borrowdale. Please see the previous page for a description

The walk falls into four distinct and well-contrasted sections:

1: to Mickleden sheepfold — easy, level walking. Gimmer Crag and Pike o' Stickle high on the right and the Band rising on the left.

2: Rossett Gill — gradual climbing, becoming steep and very stony; zig-zags preferable. Rossett's crags well seen on left, Rossett Pike on right.

3: Rossett Pass to Esk Hause — undulating grass shelf with two descents where streams flow to Langstrath, right. Esk Pike is on the left, Great End ahead and Allen Crags right.

4: Esk Hause to the summit — easy gradients, but becoming very rough across a lofty plateau; two more descents before the final steep, stony rise. Great End, right, Broad Crag, right, and Ill Crag. left. are by-passed.

NOTE
for strong walkers and supermen only:

Strong walkers may vary the return journey, *partially*, by coming back (from Esk Hause) over Esk Pike, Bowfell and the Band; or *completely* by going on to Mickledore, then down to Cam Spout, across the south edge of Esk Pike to Green Hole, up to Three Tarns and down the Band. Supermen can add to this latter walk a detour to the summit of Scafell via Lord's Rake, coming off to Cam Spout via Foxes Tarn: this involves 5,000 feet of climbing in one day, all of it rough

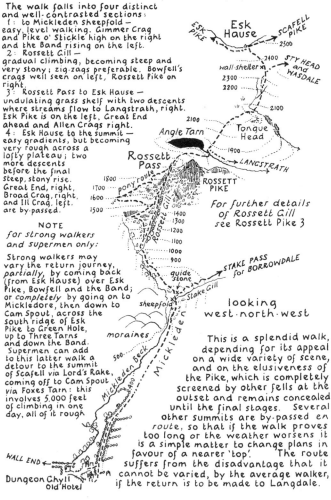

For further details of Rossett Gill see Rossett Pike 3

looking
west·north·west

This is a splendid walk, depending for its appeal on a wide variety of scene, and on the elusiveness of the Pike, which is completely screened by other fells at the outset and remains concealed until the final stages. Several other summits are by-passed en route, so that if the walk proves too long or the weather worsens it is a simple matter to change plans in favour of a nearer 'top'. The route suffers from the disadvantage that it cannot be varied, by the average walker, if the return is to be made to Langdale.

Two views
on the walk
from
Esk Hause
to the
summit

Many hearts have sunk into many boots as this
scene unfolds. Here, on the shoulder of Ill Crag,
the summit comes into sight, at last; not almost
within reach as confidently expected by walkers
who feel they have already done quite enough
to deserve success, but still a rough half-mile
distant, with two considerable descents (*Ill Crag
col and Broad Crag col*) and much climbing yet to
be faced before the goal is reached.

Bowfell

Crinkle Crags

Looking down
into Little
Narrowcove
and Eskdale,
with Ill Crag
on the left,
*from Broad
Crag col*

ASCENT FROM ESKDALE
3100 feet of ascent : 7½ miles from Boot

continued on following page

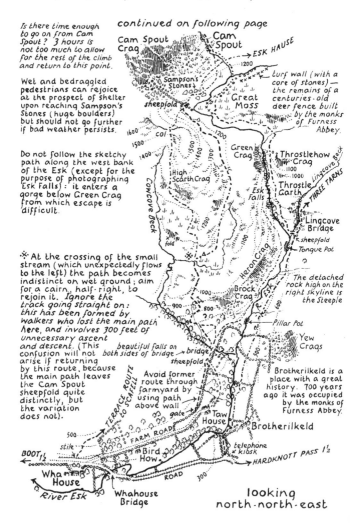

Is there time enough to go on from Cam Spout? 3 hours is not too much to allow for the rest of the climb and return to this point.

Wet and bedraggled pedestrians can rejoice at the prospect of shelter upon reaching Sampson's Stones (huge boulders) but should not go further if bad weather persists.

Do not follow the sketchy path along the west bank of the Esk (except for the purpose of photographing Esk Falls): it enters a gorge below Green Crag from which escape is difficult.

✳ At the crossing of the small stream (which unexpectedly flows to the left) the path becomes indistinct on wet ground; aim for a cairn, half-right, to rejoin it. Ignore the track going straight on: this has been formed by walkers who lost the main path here, and involves 300 feet of unnecessary ascent and descent. (This confusion will not arise if returning by this route, because the main path leaves the Cam Spout sheepfold quite distinctly, but the variation does not).

Cam Spout Crag

Cam Spout

→ ESK HAUSE
1200

turf wall (with a core of stones) — the remains of a centuries-old deer fence built by the monks of Furness Abbey.

Sampson's Stones

sheepfold

Great Moss

1600
1500
col
1400
1500
1400
1700
1200

Cowcove Beck

High Scarth Crag

1200

Green Crag
1100
1000

Throstlehow Crag

Throstle Garth

Esk Falls

Lingcove Beck

THREE TARNS

Lingcove Bridge

sheepfold
Tongue Pot

fold

✳

Heron Crag

The detached rock high on the right skyline is the Steeple

1000
900
Brock Crag
800

Pillar Pot

Yew Craggs

500

beautiful falls on both sides of bridge → bridge
sheepfold

Avoid former route through farmyard by using path above wall

TERRACE ROUTE TO SCAFELL

gate
Taw House

Brotherilkeld is a place with a great history. 700 years ago it was occupied by the monks of Furness Abbey.

Brotherilkeld

500
stile

FARM ROAD

Bird How

telephone kiosk

→ HARDKNOTT PASS 1½

BOOT 1½

Wha House

ROAD
300

River Esk

Whahouse Bridge

looking north-north-east

ASCENT FROM ESKDALE

continued

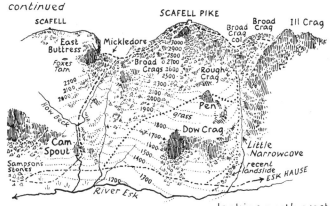

looking north-west

TO CAM SPOUT:

There is no time for dawdling when bound for Scafell Pike, and the fine high-level approach by way of Taw House and the Cowcove zigzags (avoiding the new variation *via* High Scarth Crag) is recommended as the quickest route to Cam Spout. The path from Brotherilkeld *via* Lingcove Bridge has too many distractions and temptations to halt and provides a final problem in crossing Great Moss dryshod.

FROM CAM SPOUT ONWARDS:

The usual route from Cam Spout goes up steeply by the waterfalls and proceeds thereafter on a good path, becoming a river of stones, to the ridge of Mickledore, where a well-blazed track climbs across boulders to the summit. The rock-scenery on the last stages of the struggle to Mickledore is good, Scafell East Buttress being extremely impressive, but conditions underfoot are abominable. The variation just below Mickledore that cuts off a corner and gains the ridge at its lowest point is rather easier. This route can be done in mist.

A secluded but circuitous and no less rough alternative is offered by Little Narrowcove, reached by passing below the imposing buttress of Dow Crag and completely dominated by the tremendous cliff of Ill Crag. Note the dotted line on the diagram indicating a shorter way that skirts the left edge of Dow Crag, crosses a col near the rocky peak of Pen and enters Little Narrowcove at mid-height; by careful observation it is possible, on this variation, to keep to grass all the way across the breast of the Pike. Clear weather is needed here.

It seems remarkable that England's highest mountain has no direct path to its summit on this, its finest side. It is not merely steepness that has kept walkers away from it, but rather the unavoidable, inescapable shawl of boulders covering the final 500 feet, where progress is not only painfully slow but carries a risk of displacing stones that have never before been trodden and may be balanced precariously and easily disturbed. There is no fun in pioneering routes over such rough terrain, which is safest left in virgin state.

THE SUMMIT

This is it: the Mecca of all weary pilgrims in Lakeland; the place of many ceremonies and celebrations, of bonfires and birthday parties; the ultimate; the supreme; the one objective above all others; the highest ground in England; the top of Scafell Pike.

It is a magnet, not because of its beauty for this is not a place of beauty, not because of the exhilaration of the climb for there is no exhilaration in toiling upwards over endless stones, not because of its view for although this is good there are others better. It is a magnet simply because it is the highest ground in England.

There is a huge cairn that from afar looks like a hotel: a well-built circular edifice now crumbling on its east side, with steps leading up to its flat top. Set into the vertical nine-foot north wall of the cairn is a tablet commemorating the gift of the summit to the nation. A few yards distant, west, is a triangulation column of the Ordnance Survey; a visitor in doubt and seeking confirmation of his whereabouts should consult the number on the front plate of the column: if it is anything other than S.1537 he has good cause for doubt — heaven knows where his erring steps have led him, but it is certainly not to the summit of Scafell Pike.

The surrounding area is barren, a tumbled wilderness of stones of all shapes and sizes, but it is not true, as has oft been written and may be thought, that the top is entirely devoid of vegetation: there is, indeed, a patch of grass on the south side of the cairn sufficient to provide a couch for a few hundredweights of exhausted flesh.

Yet this rough and desolate summit is, after all, just as it should be, and none of us would really want it different. A smooth green promenade here would be wrong. This is the summit of England, and it is fitting that it should be sturdy and rugged and strong.

THE SUMMIT

DESCENTS: It is an exaggeration to describe walkers' routes across the top of Scafell Pike as *paths*, because they make an uneasy pavement of angular boulders that are too unyielding ever to be trodden into subjection; nevertheless the routes are quite distinct, the particular boulders selected for their feet by the pioneers having, in the past century or so, become so extensively scratched by bootnails that they now appear as white ribbons across the grey waste of stones. Thus there is no difficulty in following them, even in mist.

The only place in descent where a walker might go astray is in going down by the Wasdale Head path to join the Corridor Route for Sty Head, the bifurcation above Lingmell col being surprisingly vague: in mist a walker might find himself well down Brown Tongue before discovering his error. It is actually safer for a stranger seeking the Corridor Route, particularly in mist, to use the Esk Hause path as far as the first col, at this point turning off *left* down into a hollow; a stream rises here and is a certain guide to the Corridor, which is reached exactly and unmistakably at the head of Piers Gill.

PLAN OF SUMMIT

Soliloquy.........

In summertime the cairn often becomes over-run with tourists, and a seeker after solitary contemplation may then be recommended to go across to the south peak, where, after enjoying the splendid view of Eskdale, he can observe the visitors to the summit from this distance. He may find himself wondering what impulse had driven these good folk to leave the comforts of the valley and make the weary ascent to this inhospitable place.

Why *does* a man climb mountains? Why has he forced his tired and sweating body up here when he might instead have been sitting at his ease in a deckchair at the seaside, looking at girls in bikinis, or fast asleep, or sucking ice-cream, according to his fancy. On the face of it the thing doesn't make sense.

Yet more and more people are turning to the hills; they find something in these wild places that can be found nowhere else. It may be solace for some, satisfaction for others: the joy of exercising muscles that modern ways of living have cramped, perhaps; or a balm for jangled nerves in the solitude and silence of the peaks; or escape from the clamour and tumult of everyday existence. It may have something to do with a man's subconscious search for beauty, growing keener as so much in the world grows uglier. It may be a need to re-adjust his sights, to get out of his own narrow groove and climb above it to see wider horizons and truer perspectives. In a few cases, it may even be a curiosity inspired by ~~awainwright's~~ Pictorial Guides. Or it may be, and for most walkers it *will* be, quite simply, a deep love of the hills, a love that has grown over the years, whatever motive first took them there: a feeling that these hills are friends, tried and trusted friends, always there when needed.

It is a question every man must answer for himself.

THE VIEW

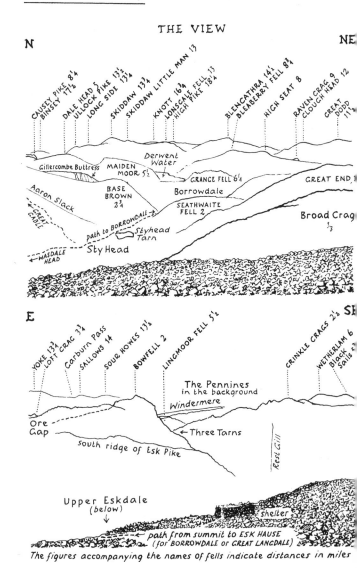

N   NE

CAUSEY PIKE 8¼
BINSEY 17½
DALE HEAD 5
ULLOCK PIKE 13½
LONG SIDE 13¼
SKIDDAW 13¾
SKIDDAW LITTLE MAN 13
KNOTT 16¾
LONSCALE FELL 13
HIGH PIKE 18¾
BLENCATHRA 14½
BLEABERRY FELL 8¾
HIGH SEAT 8
RAVEN CRAG 9
CLOUGH HEAD 12
GREAT DODD 11¼

Derwent Water

Gillercombe Buttress
MAIDEN MOOR 5½
GRANGE FELL 6¼
GREAT END

Aaron Slack
BASE BROWN 2¼
Borrowdale
GREAT GABLE
SEATHWAITE FELL 2
Broad Crag ⅓
path to BORROWDALE
Styhead Tarn
Sty Head
WASDALE HEAD

E   SE

YOKE 13¾
LOFT CRAG 3¾
Carburn Pass
SALLOWS 14
SOUR HOWES 13½
BOWFELL 2
LINGMOOR FELL 5½
CRINKLE CRAGS 2½
WETHERLAM 6
BLACK SAILS 6¼

The Pennines
in the background
Windermere

Ore Gap
← Three Tarns
south ridge of Esk Pike

Rest Gill

Upper Eskdale
(below)
shelter
← path from summit to ESK HAUSE
(for BORROWDALE or GREAT LANGDALE)

The figures accompanying the names of fells indicate distances in miles

THE VIEW

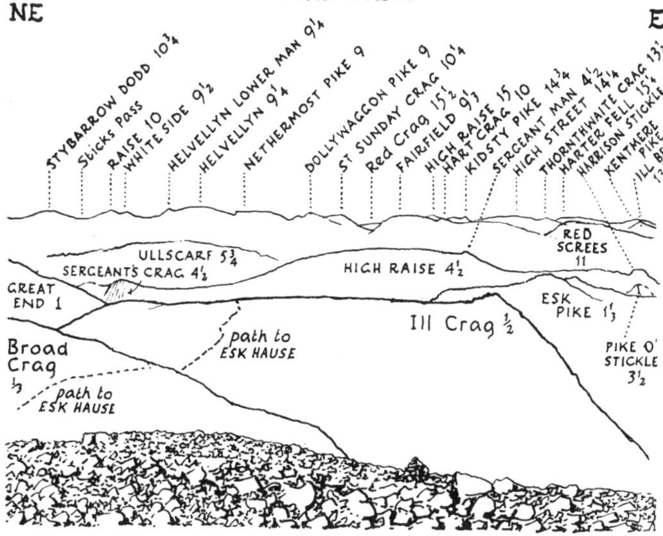
NE
E
STYBARROW DODD 10¾
Sticks Pass
RAISE 10
WHITE SIDE 9½
HELVELLYN LOWER MAN 9¼
HELVELLYN 9¼
NETHERMOST PIKE 9
DOLLYWAGGON PIKE 9
ST SUNDAY CRAG 10¼
Red Crag 15½
FAIRFIELD 9⅔
HIGH RAISE 15
HART CRAG 10
KIDSTY PIKE 14¾
SERGEANT MAN 4½
HIGH STREET 14¼
THORNTHWAITE CRAG 13½
HARTER FELL 15¼
HARRISON STICKLE 4
KENTMERE PIKE 15¼
ILL BELL 13¾
RED SCREES 11
ULLSCARF 5¾
SERGEANT'S CRAG 4½
HIGH RAISE 4½
GREAT END 1
ESK PIKE 1⅓
Ill Crag ½
path to ESK HAUSE
Broad Crag ⅓
path to ESK HAUSE
PIKE O' STICKLE 3½

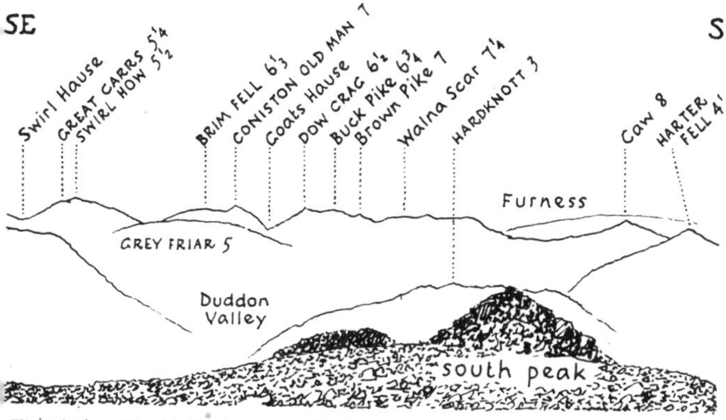
SE
S
Swirl Hause
GREAT CARRS 5¼
SWIRL HOW 5½
BRIM FELL 6⅓
CONISTON OLD MAN 7
Goats Hause
DOW CRAG 6½
Buck Pike 6¾
Brown Pike 7
Walna Scar 7¼
HARDKNOTT 3
Caw 8
HARTER FELL 4½
Furness
GREY FRIAR 5
Duddon Valley
south peak

This being the highest ground in England the view is the most extensive, although not appreciably more so than those seen from many nearby fells. There is much interesting detail in every direction, and no denying the superiority of altitude, for all else is below eye-level, with old favourites like Great Gable and Bowfell seeming, if not humbled, less proud than they usually do (Scafell, across Mickledore, often *looks* of equal or greater height). Despite the wide variety of landscape, however, this is not the most pleasing of summit views, none of the valleys or lakes in view being seen really well.

THE VIEW

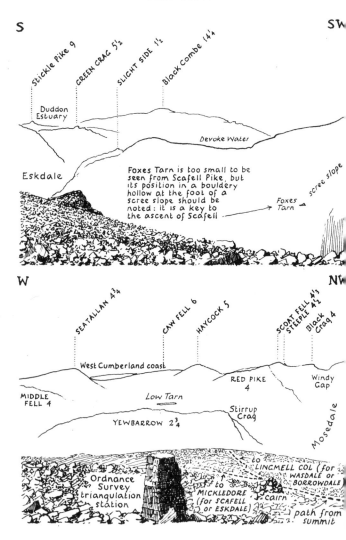

S

SW

Stickle Pike 9
GREEN CRAG 5½
SLIGHT SIDE 1½
Black Combe 14¼

Duddon
Estuary

Devoke Water

Eskdale

Foxes Tarn is too small to be
seen from Scafell Pike, but
its position in a bouldery
hollow at the foot of a
scree slope should be
noted: it is a key to
the ascent of Scafell

→ Foxes
Tarn

scree slope

W

NW

SEATALLAN 4¾
CAW FELL 6
HAYCOCK 5
SCOAT FELL 4½
STEEPLE 4½
Black Crag 4

West Cumberland coast

RED PIKE 4

Windy Gap

MIDDLE FELL 4

Low Tarn

Stirrup Crag

YEWBARROW 2¾

Mosedale

Ordnance
Survey
triangulation
station

to
MICKLEDORE
(for SCAFELL
or ESKDALE)

cairn

to
LINGMELL COL (for
WASDALE or
BORROWDALE)

path from
summit

THE VIEW

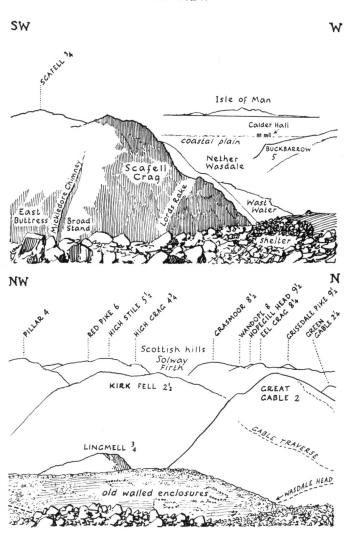

RIDGE ROUTES

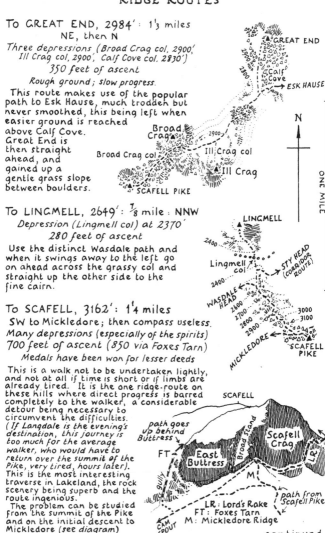

To GREAT END, 2984': 1⅓ miles
NE, then N
Three depressions (Broad Crag col, 2900', Ill Crag col, 2900', Calf Cove col, 2830')
350 feet of ascent
Rough ground; slow progress.

This route makes use of the popular path to Esk Hause, much trodden but never smoothed, this being left when easier ground is reached above Calf Cove. Great End is then straight ahead, and gained up a gentle grass slope between boulders.

To LINGMELL, 2649': ⅞ mile : NNW
Depression (Lingmell col) at 2370'
280 feet of ascent

Use the distinct Wasdale path and when it swings away to the left go on ahead across the grassy col and straight up the other side to the fine cairn.

To SCAFELL, 3162': 1¼ miles
SW to Mickledore; then compass useless.
Many depressions (especially of the spirits)
700 feet of ascent (850 via Foxes Tarn)
Medals have been won for lesser deeds

This is a walk not to be undertaken lightly, and not at all if time is short or if limbs are already tired. It is the one ridge-route on these hills where direct progress is barred completely to the walker, a considerable detour being necessary to circumvent the difficulties. (*If Langdale is the evening's destination, this journey is too much for the average walker, who would have to return over the summit of the Pike, very tired, hours later*). This is the most interesting traverse in Lakeland, the rock scenery being superb and the route ingenious.

The problem can be studied from the summit of the Pike and on the initial descent to Mickledore (*see diagram*)

path goes up behind Buttress

LR : Lord's Rake
FT : Foxes Tarn
M : Mickledore Ridge

path from Scafell Pike

continued

RIDGE ROUTES

To SCAFELL (continued)

Lord's Rake
(top of first section)

Lord's Rake
as seen from
Mickledore

On the way down to Mickledore it appears that the route must continue up the narrow slope directly beyond it, *but this is Broad Stand: no way here.* A choice must be made between the two pedestrian routes *via* Lord's Rake or Foxes Tarn. For Lord's Rake, which is recommended, go to the far end of Mickledore Ridge and (after agreeing that Broad Stand is impossible) slither to the right down scree to a path that runs below the crags to the foot of Lord's Rake (now see Scafell 4 and 9 for details). For Foxes Tarn, descend *left* (path) from the near end of Mickledore Ridge to join the main path for Cam Spout but leave this 150 yards lower and enter and ascend a gully on the right to a small pond: this is Foxes Tarn. Steep scree, right, leads up to the top.

And the best of luck...

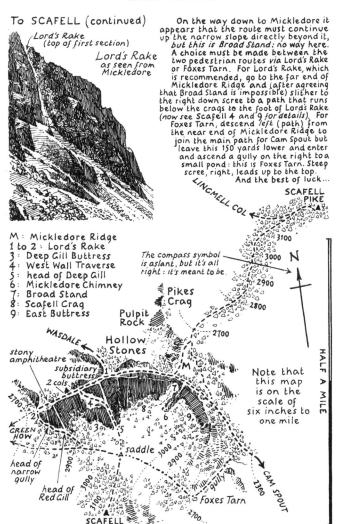

M : Mickledore Ridge
1 to 2 : Lord's Rake
3 : Deep Gill Buttress
4 : West Wall Traverse
5 : head of Deep Gill
6 : Mickledore Chimney
7 : Broad Stand
8 : Scafell Crag
9 : East Buttress

The compass symbol is aslant, but it's all right : it's meant to be

Note that this map is on the scale of six inches to one mile

LINGMELL COL

SCAFELL PIKE

3100
3000
2900
N
2800
2700

HALF A MILE

Pikes Crag
Pulpit Rock
WASDALE
Hollow Stones

stony amphitheatre
subsidiary buttress
2 cols

2700

GREEN HOW

saddle

head of narrow gully

2900

3000
3100

SCAFELL

head of Red Gill

2900

Foxes Tarn

2700

CAM SPOUT

2300

POSTSCRIPT: A PASTIME FOR LIFE
from The Outlying Fells of Lakeland

WALK : *The ordinary human gait in which both feet are never off the ground at once.*

WALKING : *The act of going on foot : act of moving with a slow step.*

These are dictionary definitions. They make no reference to the pleasures that can accrue from walking, no mention of the beneficial exercise so gained nor of the satisfaction felt upon reaching a desired objective on foot under your own steam.

Walking comes naturally to all of us. We walk (by roundabout routes) from cradle to grave. For most people walking is, throughout life, a simple means of locomotion from point A to point B, and preferably by the shortest and easiest route. If a car comes along they hop in; might as well save their legs, they say.

A minority, however, walk for pleasure, finding enjoyment as they go along, exploring old haunts and visiting new scenes, developing an awareness of the things around them. Some have a burning curiosity to look round the next corner and some find a supreme joy in attaining remote places.

The best walking is the traversing of terrain that can only be reached on foot, and in country with a crowded network of roads on lower ground this means walking on hills and moorlands that are inaccessible to wheeled traffic and where the only method of progress is by use of the legs — lonely country, inevitably: natural wildernesses where most people wouldn't be seen dead, so they say, and certainly not alive. Walkers who walk for the sake of walking are still, by many people, regarded as crackpots.

This sort of rough tramping has become known, in the last century, as fellwalking. It is not a game, not a sport, not a competing with others, but a pastime: a simple way of spending leisure hours alone or in the company of kindred beings that has as its aim merely the study of nature in some form or other: flora or fauna, geology, the lie of the land; or of sites of antiquarian interest on the hills: old mine-workings, relics of former civilisations, ancient settlements. All harmless pursuits, all instructive. Most fellwalkers become aware of the fascination of these 'sideline' interests but the over-riding impulse generally is to reach a pre-determined objective. The objective is usually a mountain top. Mountain tops are very satisfying. They are well-defined landmarks, usually indicated by a cairn. They are attained only after exercise of the limbs, the satisfaction of surmounting them being in direct proportion to the effort involved — the harder the task the greater the reward, which is as it should be. They are remote, detached from everyday life. They are new viewpoints, reminders of true values, places to refresh the soul, to banish worries, to sweep away the cobwebs that so confuse the urban mind. In a changing world they remain unchanged. In the modern swirl of shifting and transient loyalties they are anchors. One always feels better after climbing a mountain.

Fellwalking is a pastime available to everyone, and unlike games and sports is not restricted to age groups. It is a pastime for the young and the middle-aged and the old; indeed, its attractions actually increase as the years go by. Ardent fellwalkers never give up. They fade away, in due course, surrounded by maps, their gnarled fingers still tracing fresh routes. They die hoping for hills in heaven.

White hair is no deterrent. Retirement from the factory or office is not an end to everything: it is not an end to anything but work. Fellwalking helps better than doctors to keep a man fit, and enthusiastic not only about hills but about life... The satisfaction derived from a successful climb becomes even keener with the passing years.

Fellwalking is a pastime for life.

I suppose it might be said, to add impressiveness to the whole thing, that this book has been twenty years in the making, for it is so long, and more, since I first came from a smoky mill-town (forgive me, Blackburn!) and beheld, from Orrest Head, a scene of great beauty, a fascinating paradise, Lakeland's mountains and trees and water. That was the first time I had looked upon beauty, or imagined it, even. Afterwards I went often, whenever I could, and always my eyes were lifted to the hills. I was to find then, and it has been so ever since, a spiritual and physical satisfaction in climbing mountains — and a tranquil mind upon reaching their summits, as though I had escaped from the disappointments and unkindnesses of life and emerged above them into a new world, a better world.

But that is by the way. In those early Lakeland days I served my apprenticeship faithfully, learning all the time. At first, the hills were frightening, moody giants, and I a timid Gulliver, but very gradually through the years we became acquaintances and much later firm friends.

In due course I came to live within sight of the hills, and I was well content. If I could not be climbing, I was happy to sit idly and dream of them, serenely. Then came a restlessness and the feeling that it was not enough to take their gifts and do nothing in return. I must dedicate something of myself, the best part of me, to them. I started to write about them, and to draw pictures of them. Doing these things, I found they were still giving and I still receiving, for a great pleasure filled me when I was so engaged — I had found a new way of escape to them and from all else less worth while.

Thus it comes about that I have written this book. Not for material gain, welcome though that would be (you see I have not escaped entirely!); not for the benefit of my contemporaries, though if it brings them also to the hills I shall be well pleased; certainly not for posterity, about which I can work up no enthusiasm at all. No, this book has been written, carefully and with infinite patience, for my own pleasure and because it has seemed to bring the hills to my own fireside. If it has merit, it is because the hills have merit.

I started the book determined that everything in it should be perfect, with the consequence that I spent the first six months filling wastepaper baskets. Only then did I accept what I should have known and acknowledged from the start — that nothing created by man is perfect, or can hope to be; and having thus consoled and cheered my hurt conceit I got along like a house on fire. So let me be the first to say it: this book is full of imperfections. But let me dare also to say that (apart from many minor blemishes of which I am already deeply conscious and have no wish to be reminded) it is free from inaccuracies.